Scotland's Greatest Mysteries

RICHARD WILSON

D1380267

LOMOND

First Published in the UK in 2019 by

Lomond Books Ltd
13-14 Freskyn Place
East Mains Industrial Estate
Broxburn
EH52 5NF

www.lomondbooks.co.uk

ISBN 978-1-84204-669-2

A CIP record of this book is available
from the British Library.

Printed and bound by MBM Print SCS Ltd, Glasgow

Contents

To my wife Ali, the greatest Scottish mystery of all.

1

A Monster Mystery

WHAT ON EARTH is it and why, after nearly 15 centuries of allegedly being sighted in and around the deep waters of Loch Ness, has it never been fully exposed to public scrutiny?

Is the oft-claimed existence of the world's most famous monster just wishful thinking? 'While there are many people who do not believe it exists,' wrote Daniel Cohen in his book *A Modern Look at Monsters*, 'there is practically no-one who would not be overjoyed to find out that it did.'

Despite hundreds of claimed sightings and more than a few photos, films and videos of an animate presence in the 36-kilometre-long loch that slices diagonally through Scotland's central Highlands, nothing physical or tangible has ever emerged through its peat-darkened waters to remove the scepticism or derision that greets true believers. No pieces of skin, no half-eaten remnants of prey, not even – despite its having apparently been seen on land – a footprint. Not a real one anyway...

Employing primitive box cameras, then deep-sea divers and underwater television, then today's super-sophisticated technology, since the 1930s there have been no fewer than ten expeditions mounted, with various degrees of imagination, in pursuit of the monster. Perhaps the most impressive were those of the Loch Ness Investigation Bureau founded in 1962. They featured searchlights, echo sounders, airborne searches, hot-air balloons, sonar systems, infra-red cameras and submarines and had the support of Sir Peter Scott, renowned naturalist, broadcaster, artist, and then-president of the World Wildlife Fund.

Though his investigation bureau closed in 1972 through lack of funds, its sonar systems twice produced 'large, strong contacts' around the loch, and four years later Sir Peter wrote a convincing piece in *Wildlife* magazine entitled 'Why I Believe in Nessie'. It was backed by the famous close-up photo supposedly of Nessie's 'flipper' that resulted from the bureau's metaphorical baton being grasped by the underwater photography operation of Robert Rines' Boston-based Academy of Applied Science – a picture that first tantalised but gradually lost credibility due to suspected retouching.

Not even the 1987 Operation Deep Scan, that deployed 19 lined-up cruisers with echo-sounding devices, has delivered a result that would make the world sit up and acknowledge the definite presence of an unknown beast in the largest and second deepest (220 metres) of the three Ice Age lochs in the Great Glen Fault.

Surely the only thing for it, then, is to turn to the late Sir Peter's like-minded friend of wildlife, now the world's most celebrated authority in that field; the man who tracked down Indonesia's Komodo dragons; the man with today's most respected word on earth, literally – Sir David Attenborough.

'People of a certain age remember me for *Fabulous Animals*, a programme I made about mythical beasts and mysterious creatures like the Yeti and the Loch Ness monster,' he told *Esquire* magazine in 2014. 'But do I believe in such things? Come on – I think we're all too grown-up to believe that there's a Loch Ness monster.'

Could he possibly have been misquoted? Surely this man, who has seen so many of the Earth's miraculous life forms, must accept there is still much that even he has not yet seen?

I resolved to ask him again, just to get it right. To a good old-fashioned handwritten enquiry, he replied promptly from his base in Richmond in his own, good old-fashioned handwriting, 'Dear Rick Wilson: *Of course* the Nessie story is a hoax.'

But why would such an elaborate hoax be perpetrated so persistently over so many years? The stock modern answer is, to attract the tourists. That obviously couldn't have been the case at the first recorded sighting in 565 AD by the Irish missionary Saint Columba, who reportedly saw a follower being threatened, while trying to retrieve a boat, by a strange beast that had already killed a Pict and was apparently still hungry. It had been 'lurking in the depths of the river, keen for more prey... and with a mighty roar from its gaping mouth, sped towards the man' – until the saint pulled off a famous miracle by banishing it with 'the saving sign of the cross'.

It can't be denied, however, that the area's ongoing subliminal 'here be monsters' message pulls curious people from all over the world, to the value of some £30million a year if it's assumed that each one of 300,000 visitors spends around £100 locally, between Inverness at the top of the loch and Fort Augustus at its foot; and that two rival Nessie exhibitions in Drumnadrochit on its western edge act as magnets for visitors who can at least console themselves that if they don't see the real thing, they somehow got closer to it through the pictures and models.

It also can't be denied that among the early 1970s estimate of over 10,000 sightings across the years and centuries there have been many deliberate attempts to deceive. Indeed, later in that decade the figure for documented sightings was revised to about 3,000, which, because there could be many well-meaning but doubtful and even deceitful claims, was then hacked down by Chicago University's Professor Roy Mackal to less than 300 'valid' reports.

We can at least conclude from such an exercise that there have been many, many more 'invalid' sightings than ones to be taken seriously. And Sir David clearly believes there is no point in pursuing the legend in the vain hope that it might be real.

The words 'end of story' did not conclude his note, but they might as well have. Yet one hopes the great man doesn't mind if the question keeps nagging. The story goes on for the veritable army of something-spotters. Another expert whose word is well worthy of attention, Gary Campbell is a chartered accountant based in Inverness and working, in his day job, for the University of the Highlands and Islands. His other vocation, which he has practised since 1996, is being official registrar of Loch Ness sightings of unusual shapes and movements – he hesitates to say 'monsters' as such – witnessed on the surface of the loch, often by people who were not previous subscribers to the idea.

He himself is one such. Which is why, soon after a catalytic experience in 1996, he set up the Official Loch Ness Monster Sightings Register, realising that there was no central agency collating and controlling sightings. 'Though I come from this area, I never really believed in the monster story. It wasn't any kind of boyhood fantasy for me. I was just as sceptical as anyone else, with no thoughts one way or the other, but then when I was parked in a lay-by at the side of the loch doing some paperwork, I sensed a bit of commotion and I couldn't believe my eyes when I looked up to see this black hump coming out of the water just in front of me; not once but twice. It seemed smaller than a whale but bigger than a seal. And then it just disappeared.'

The scene had a profound effect on him, to the extent that

he now devotes much of his life to running 'the only place that lists every Nessie sighting'...with the ultimate objective of finding out what 'it' is, though he does admit, 'It's so elusive I expect I'll be doing this till the day I die.' He sees that all credible sightings are now properly registered and all photographic evidence strictly vetted. That has become relatively easier in recent years, he says, with the advent of the ubiquitous phone-camera's instant capacity to capture a moment or even video a sequence of movements. 'It means we can quickly check provenance and discount the unlikely ones.'

Despite the impact of what he witnessed, he does not call himself a monster-believer, though he is convinced there is 'something' there: 'I don't know what it is, but I'm intrigued and looking for the answer like everyone else.'

He is fairly sure the word 'monster' takes people, including serious scientists, on a misleading trail. 'Monster was the rather creative label that the editor of the *Inverness Courier* put on it to add drama to a sighting report in the 1930s,' he says, 'and the national and international press picked it up with relish. To the extent that the label has never been shaken off.'

He is talking about the birth of the modern Nessie legend, when a sighting made local news on 2 May 1933. The Inverness paper told the story of a local couple, John and Aldie Mackay, who claimed to have seen 'an enormous animal like a whale rolling and plunging on the surface' near Abriachan Pier. The editor's headline-grabbing word of choice prompted London newspapers to send reporters to Scotland on a wild monster chase, while a circus offered a £20,000 reward for anyone capturing the beast.

Those sensation-seekers who persevered were not to be totally disappointed, as another sighting within three months fed into the growing Nessie fever that was attracting sightseers from all over the country. On July 22 another couple, the Spicers, a tailoring family from London, claimed to have seen the beast on land, crossing the road in front of their open-topped Austin convertible. It was, they said, 'a most extraordinary form of animal (…) an abomination and a loathsome sight'.

In November of the same year, Hugh Gray, a respected local employee of the British Aluminium Company, photographed a 20 foot 'serpent' off Foyers and claimed the result was the first-ever image of the monster. He told a Scottish national paper:

> Four Sundays ago, after church, I went for my usual walk near where the river enters the loch. The loch was like a mill pond and the sun shining brightly. An object of con-siderable dimensions rose out of the water not very far from where I was. I immediately got my camera ready and snapped the object which was two or three feet above the surface of the water. I did not see any head, for what I took to be the front parts were under the water, but there was considerable movement from what seemed to be the tail, the part furthest from me. The object only appeared for a few minutes then sank out of sight.

In the near-century since then, some people claim to have seen the monster multiple times – five, in the case of Mrs J Simpson of Alltsigh – while other determined types have been deeply disappointed, such as Bournemouth-born Steve Feltham who spent 28 years camped on the side of the loch without seeing anything other than 'a rolling wave'.

So what could it possibly be? There have been enough ideas from amateurs and professionals to fill the rest of this chapter, but here is a modest selection – giant eel, Wels catfish, large bearded seal, overgrown salamander, small whale, black swan, algal slime nourished by sewage, odd-shaped tree trunk, swimming dog, gigantic iguana, African lungfish, grouped otters, vegetation mat, sea serpent, merganser duck, giant squid, legendary horse-shaped kelpie, upturned boat, and – most intriguingly – plesiosaur, a marine reptile last seen on earth 60 million years ago and assumed (by some) to have been trapped in the loch by the ancient geological movements that created it. There have also been sudden waves and boat wakes on the loch's surface that (for some) have created scary pictures and even real tragic events – the car-racing hero John Cobb died here in 1952 when, in an attempt at the water speed record, his boat struck an unexplained wake.

A great believer in the plesiosaur theory was Constance Whyte, a local doctor and one of the Loch Ness Investigation Bureau's three founders, who in 1957 wrote a book entitled *More Than A Legend*, which explosively re-ignited fading interest in the Nessie legend carrying, as it did, several pictures of the beast and the concluding assertion that 'There is a real monster in Loch Ness'. What made her so sure?

> The evidence rests on the testimony of hundreds of witnesses of integrity. My hope is that the evidence will now be accepted in spite of the many theoretical difficulties.
>
> What the monster is, no-one knows, or can know with any degree of certainty until there has been a thorough scientific investigation. In fairness to those who, in the face of ridicule and worse, have held publicly to what they know to be true, I hope the case for a large live monster at home in Loch Ness will now be found proven.

Here are a couple of the numerous witness quotes she recounted.

Miss E McG, a Fort Augustus resident, was crossing Oich bridge when she:

> saw three stationary humps which later began to move forward with some up-and-down undulating movement but on a straight course. Then a long, snake-like neck appeared and the monster set off suddenly at a fast speed towards Borlum Bay, where it seemed to play about on the surface for about ten minutes, after which it disappeared.

Mr D Mackenzie of Caberfeidh, Balnain, by Loch Ness, wrote in 1934:

> I saw it at about 12 o'clock on a grand sunny day, so that it was impossible to be mistaken. It seemed to me to be rather like an upturned boat [but] it went at great speed, wriggling and churning up the water. I have told the same story to my friends long before the present monster became famous.

Unfortunately, among her presented evidence of photos and colourful accounts by such witnesses of integrity, Dr Whyte posthumously fell victim to the worst hoax ever committed in the name of the would-be monster, as she died in 1982 before it was accepted as a fake.

There have been many Nessie hoaxes, such as the case of the crocodile claw found close to Urquhart Castle, the planted trail of prints from the left hind foot of a hippopotamus, a brown bear's skull discovered on the loch's shore, and the world-circulated photo faked by local skipper George Edwards 'for a bit of fun'. Campbell's website devotes a whole section to such malicious or playful aberrations. But by far the most blatant intention to deceive – which fooled the world for 60 years – was the so-called Surgeon's Photograph that was given critical credence in all three editions of Dr Whyte's book (and is reproduced on the front cover of this one) despite her growing suspicions of it latterly.

It became clear in 1994 that this picture, which had become the most iconic image of the Loch Ness Monster, showing head and neck rising from the water – was, in fact, a fake. It was identified by the word 'surgeon' because it was supposedly taken by someone so respectable he refused to have his name attached to it – Robert Kenneth Wilson, a London gynaecologist who apparently liked a practical joke and had been enlisted to give the hoax credence. It was first published in the monster-believing *Daily Mail* to which he gave this account of his (not so) big moment:

I decided to come and spend a few days at the place to see what it was like out of the shooting season, and to try to get some photographs of wild fowl – and trains. To this end I borrowed a quarter-plate camera with a telephoto lens. I was inexperienced as a photographer and was, in fact, very much of the amateur… At about 7 or 7.30am I stopped by the roadside two or three miles on the Inverness side of Invermoriston at a point where the road is some feet above the loch… I got over the dyke and was standing a few yards down the slope and looking towards the loch when I noticed a considerable commotion on the surface, some distance out from the shore, perhaps two or three hundred yards out. When I had watched it for perhaps a minute or so, something broke surface and I saw the head of some strange animal rising out of the water.

I hurried to the car for my camera then went down and

along the steep bank for about 50 yards to get a better view and focused on something which was moving through the water. I was too busy managing the camera to make accurate observation but I made four exposures, by which time the object had completely disappeared. I had no idea at the time whether I had anything on the plates or not, but thought I might have.

All of which was nonsense. He had simply been a messenger for the hoaxers. Suspicions were initially aroused in a 1975 *Sunday Telegraph* piece. By 1994 it had been fairly well established that the photo was an elaborate fake; and in 1999 details of how it came about were published in David Martin and Alastair Boyd's *Nessie: The Surgeon's Photograph Exposed*.

It revealed that the 'creature' was in fact a Woolworth's toy submarine creatively disguised by model-maker Christian Spurling, the son-in-law of Marmaduke Wetherell, who had been ridiculed by his employer, the *Daily Mail*, after his acclaimed find of Nessie footprints turned out to be false. With the help of his son Ian and insurance agent Maurice Chambers, the hoax was mounted as an act of revenge. Wetherell Jnr took the photos near the Altsaigh Tea House and, when he heard a water bailiff approaching, pushed the model under the water with his foot.

Chambers then gave the photographic plates to Wilson, who took them to Ogston's, an Inverness chemist, where he was excitedly advised that the print was so sensational it should go to the national press such as the *Mail*. And the rest, as they say, is history.

The offending model might still be stuck on the loch's bed, and probably more easy to find than the 'real' thing. If that exists at all, he or she is frustratingly elusive. But in 2015, Gary Campbell accepted five sightings, and 11 were logged in 2017, the most in 13 years. It has been a long haul for him, however. After ploughing through news reports for the 'missing decade' as he calls it – 1985-1996 – he has recorded to date over a thousand modern examples of 'possibly believable' sightings of 'something' in the vast loch that contains more fresh water than all the lakes in England and Wales combined. These days, when claimed sightings are backed with discussable evidence, spotters are expected to fill in a form he publishes on the web with time-and-place details ('Please describe your sighting giving estimates of size, distance, colour of object').

He has also taken on the additional task of recording other sightings elsewhere in Scotland, where there are no fewer than 23 other lochs said to host large unknown creatures. But Scotland is not alone. There are records – kept elsewhere, to his relief – of several other such monstrous creatures across the world. Apart from known-to-be-real examples, such as the elusive Greenland shark and the now-extinct Behring's Sea Cow once found in Canada's Henry Island, there are the more mysterious ones such as Congo's Mokele-mbembe; the USA's Champ, said to live in Lake Champlain; Canada's Ogopogo, inhabitant of the Okanagan Lake in British Columbia; and a lake monster called Nahuelito reportedly living in Patagonia's Nahuel Huapi Lake. All of which can boast long histories of being spotted by locals and visitors alike…

None of which helps us to know exactly what such a beast might look like. In Nessie's case, there are conflicting stories of its coils and bumps and skin colours and a gargoyle head 'with wicked pig-like eyes', often adding up to the 'loathsome sight' seen by George Spicer; but perhaps the most trustable image is that painted by Sir Peter Scott, of a pair of monsters swimming under water looking benign, devoted and very similar to what's known of the ancient plesiosaur. This was backed up, incidentally, by schoolchildren at Drumnadrochit in the 1930s who, when asked by their teacher to describe the 'horrifying' animal they had spotted in the swampy shallows of Urquhart Bay, pointed without hesitation to the picture of the plesiosaur displayed on their classroom wall.

Yet still the hunt goes on for this elusive creature. The summer of 2018 saw a team of water-borne researchers engaged in a super-modern scientific method of trying to find it – namely, the taking of loch water samples from which (hopefully) picked-up traces of left-behind animal and fish DNA would be the key. Extracted in the lab, it would be compared against a list of known species. The team leader, Professor Neil Gemmell of the University of Otago in New Zealand said: 'Our project is fundamentally seeking to document the biodiversity of Loch Ness and in so doing we may find evidence of a monster. But we won't hold our breath.' Indeed, they moved on without a sensational discovery...

Another university expert to grapple recently with the enigma of the monster is Gareth Williams, Emeritus Professor and former Dean of Medicine at the University of Bristol. His book *A Monstrous Commotion, the Mysteries of Loch Ness* is a super-deep loch of research which adds much to its own bibliography of 46 Nessie books published over the century. Seven websites on the subject are also mentioned. And when you add his so-comprehensive story to all the years of news reports, photos, films, television documentaries, scientific expeditions, on-the-line academic reputations, and general worldwide enthralment about a thing that may not even exist, you have to ask: How is *that* possible? That so much fuss can come from nothing? So...

Having devoted more brain power to the question than anyone else in recent times, does Professor Williams now believe in the monster's existence? His book's penultimate sentence doesn't quite reveal his position: 'It's a great story and I hope I've done it justice.' Its last thought gives a clearer hint: 'Loch Ness is vast and impenetrable, and a place where almost anything could be hiding.'

But can he do better? We contact him directly at his Gloucestershire home and ask the question bluntly: 'Do you now believe?' He seems to smile into the phone as he says:

If you put me against a wall and forced me to a conclusion, I'd have to say [long hesitation] the possibility can't be excluded. Many people have seen something, no doubt about that. But I think the Nessie story has been embroidered by the imagination of people – including many respectable and diligent scientists – honestly excited by the unknown. And no-one would be more delighted than me if they proved there was something there.

You might almost think he believes…

2

Crusoe's Lost Papers

DANIEL DEFOE WAS a man of many parts – pamphleteer, tax inspector, journalist, economist, merchant, spy, and – most brilliantly of all – author of one of the world's celebrated and long-lived novels, *Robinson Crusoe*. Written around 300 years ago, it has been a best-seller over all that time, and when – to illustrate that point – this writer checked out its availability in a bookshop in Bristol, where his killer quill got the vital spark for the thing, there were five different versions on sale ... two for grown-ups and three for children, who, according to the manager, 'often appreciate it more than contemporary stories'.

Quite a best-selling success story, then, for a work of fiction. The only trouble with that sentence being that it is not *really* entirely fiction. It has long been generally presumed that, although most of the Crusoe book was certainly made up, the basic story was that of the Scottish sailor Alexander Selkirk, whose experience of being marooned on a remote Chilean island, Juan Fernandez, provided the inspiration, framework and all the essential detail.

Selkirk's captain on his return journey, Woodes Rogers, had written about rescuing the young (but old-looking) mariner after four and a half years, recalling his crew's amazement at finding 'a Man cloth'd in Goat-Skins who look'd wilder than the first Owners of them'. The account had caused such a wave of interest in London and beyond that Defoe, always alert to the main chance, would not have missed it; and consequently wondered how he could hitch a ride with it to his own advantage. It would, of course, require an interview or two with the now famous but broadly spoken navigator, from Lower Largo in Fife. And surely he would understand him better than the average Englishman would? Defoe had been, after all, an Edinburgh-based English government spy reporting on the Scots' machinations before the 1707 Union; then editor of the *Edinburgh Courant* working from his Moubray House home (built in 1462 and still standing next to the John Knox House halfway down the Royal Mile). His ear would thus have been well tuned to Selkirk's east coast Scottish accent.

Up to that point, Defoe as a father of seven children, had been in dire straits despite his obvious talents. He had embarked into fiction in his late 50s, broke and struggling to find rewarding work for which no magic key was provided by his track record as a prolific and versatile writer, having produced more than 500 books, pamphlets and journals on topics including politics, crime, religion, marriage, geography and psychology. None of these journalistic or literary efforts had delivered him much financial security. Indeed, he often got into serious trouble – such as bankruptcy and imprisonment – because of his political intensity, his tendency to libel people, and his inability to stay out of debt.

So it must have been an immeasurable relief to him when the publication of *Robinson Crusoe* created a sensation in London and beyond. Published in 1719, the novel was a huge and immediate success. Everything about it seemed to be record-breaking, including its full title: *The Life and Strange Surprizing Adventures of Robinson Crusoe, of York, Mariner; Who lived Eight and Twenty Years, all alone in an un-inhabited Island on The Coast of AMERICA, near the Mouth of the Great River Oroonoque […] An Account how he was at last as strangely delivered by Pyrates.*

21

It was soon referred to simply as *Robinson Crusoe*, of course, and before the end of the year the first edition had run through four print runs. As is so often the case with blockbusters, many publishers had turned it down. But William Taylor, the one who accepted it, soon found demand so great he had to employ several printers simultaneously to keep up. Often said to be the first English novel, *Robinson Crusoe* had, within a few years, reached a readership as wide as any book ever written in that language. By the end of the 19th century it had been published in at least 700 editions and translations. And it has remained enduringly popular throughout the world ever since. It is still the most widely read book after the Bible, has been translated into virtually every known tongue, and sold tens of millions of copies.

Despite that huge achievement, Defoe made surprisingly little money out of it as he sold the copyright and still managed to die poor, probably hiding from his creditors. But in the creation of *Crusoe* he hit a rich vein of abiding human curiosity. The idea of being separated from civilised society and having to fend for yourself all alone on a deserted island has universal appeal. We all wonder how we would fare in such circumstances. Would we go berserk, jump off a cliff from which we see no rescue ships, or buckle down and apply some practical self-discipline to the challenge and wait it out?

Selkirk was one man who had really lived it, and the only person shy about acknowledging his input was Defoe himself. It seems Selkirk experienced a fair mix of these reactions, which no doubt gave Defoe convincingly authentic detail to work on. But did he get it second-hand or from the man himself? The author denied ever meeting Selkirk, but there has long been a huge question mark over that. At the very least there were two others known to both Defoe and Selkirk who certainly influenced the creation of *Crusoe* – the rescue tale-teller Captain Woodes Rogers and the London journalist and essayist Richard Steele, who had interviewed the Scot for *The Englishman* magazine. Their well-circulated and avidly-read accounts of the castaway's adventures surely excited Defoe, who was a friend of Steele, and the two writers must surely have discussed the whole castaway saga together.

Defoe was obviously taken by the 'novel' potential of the tale and (it is respectfully suggested) set about getting his own first-hand, horse's-mouth interview with Selkirk who, after his return to England in 1711 with a hugely bountiful Spanish treasure ship, spent some time in Bristol awaiting another ambitious voyage with Captain Rogers. Indeed, the captain brought Selkirk into his Bristol home in leafy, elegant Queen Square partly to reserve and prepare him for this voyage – with a new South Sea Company – and partly to show him off as something of a promotional novelty to augment the undoubted impact of his (the captain's) book, *A Cruising Voyage round the World*.

'A bizarre story is told,' recalls the *Western Daily Press* feature writer and editor Gerry Brooke, 'that while he was a guest of Woodes Rogers, Selkirk amused the local gentry by parading round the elegant square on a Sunday after church, decked out in his island goatskins.'

While Selkirk was becoming a local hero of sorts, Defoe was a frequent visitor to Bristol – wearing another of his many hats as a government excise commissioner for glass duty, responsible for collecting the tax on bottle manufacture. But his writer's hat was never far from his head. Had he heard from someone that Selkirk had 'papers' – presumably some kind of invaluable log of his adventure? Contrary to Defoe's own denial, there is some evidence to suggest that he did talk to Selkirk – several times in a few different places – and that he took 'papers' from him. If he did not then return them, that would have been potentially scandalous and perhaps might explain his denial of a meeting.

Another theory is advanced by Bristol historian Mark Steeds:

> I believe Defoe denied having contact with Selkirk because he wanted to distance himself from him so that *Robinson Crusoe* would be perceived as all his own unassisted work.

In any case, it is quite widely accepted in Bristol that Defoe and Selkirk met in the picturesque Tudor-style Llandoger Trow pub, a place which propels you magically back to the 18th century while gracing King Street at right angles to the Welsh Back quayside that saw much River Avon traffic from Wales. On a sumptuously carved period wooden mantelpiece, the pub boasts a pillar that stakes the claim:

> The Llandoger Trow dates back to 1664 and is steeped in history and legend, the most famous of which are the literary connections to Daniel Defoe and Robert Louis Stevenson. It is said that Daniel Defoe met Alexander Selkirk, the marooned sailor on which he based the book Robinson Crusoe, here.

It is a convincing olde worlde atmosphere and therefore very tempting to picture the two men huddled by candlelight in a corner of the pub – and to believe the bald statement on another of its wall mountings: 'Many famous people have visited here and there appears to be no question that this is where Alexander Selkirk met Daniel Defoe of Robinson Crusoe fame.' But pinning down the meeting place is not quite as simple as that. 'There were a couple of pubs off Castle Street that had better claims,' says Gerry Brooke, who is an enthusiastic member of the local Long John Silver Trust, which studies and promotes Bristol's maritime history, 'but unfortunately they're long gone.'

Historian Steeds, an equally energetic member of the trust, agrees:

> Despite Defoe's recorded denial, I think the two men definitely met – and probably a few times. Selkirk wasn't always at Woodes Rogers' house and when he lodged at the Cock and Bottle Inn in the lane of the same name off Castle Street there was a pub there called *The Star* where Defoe stayed. It seems to me quite probable that they met in the latter, which was known for its convivial wit.
>
> I think it is almost impossible that the two men could not have known each other. How could they have avoided meeting each other in the same street?

Not only that. Meetings between the two were also said to have taken place in a private house in Bristol – that of Mrs Damaris [or Daniel] in St James Square, and Steeds claims there were sworn affidavits by witnesses 'who saw Defoe take Selkirk's papers away'.

That there were indeed Selkirk 'papers' seems to be confirmed by a visit to Bristol Central Library where this writer found the following 'Evidence of the meeting of Alexander Selkirk and Daniel Defoe' on a couple of faded typewritten sheets with the prompting of a yellowing card-indexing system in a venerable wallside cabinet. Extract from *The Bristol Mirror,* dated Saturday, 1 March, 1851:

Sir, – Having accidentally taken up an old paper of yours (October 20th, 1849), I found it stated, in a very interesting account of the Duke and Dutchess privateers, that my grandfather, Alderman Harford, 'was the first person who proved that De Foe composed Robinson Crusoe from papers given him by Alexander Selkirk' and that you would be glad of any further information on the subject.

I have much pleasure in confirming the account there given, having often heard my father say that 'an old lady [Mrs Daniel, a daughter of the celebrated Major Wade] told my grandfather that Selkirk had informed her that he had placed his papers in De Foe's hands'.

My grandfather purchased many of the things which were sold on the return of the Duke and Dutchess, with the rich prize of the Manilla ship (mentioned by Woodes Rogers in his account of the voyage, in which Selkirk was found, on the island of Juan Fernandez); they are now in my possession, and consist principally of very handsome china, which was going to the Queen of Spain, with curious articles, in tortoise shell and Indian ink. Captain Rogers [then] lived at Frenchay, in the house now the residence of Mrs Brice.

I am, Sir, your obedient servant,
Henry Charles Harford

[The Harfords were a prominent Bristol banking family.]

Further sources suggest Selkirk did indeed have 'papers' and undertook meetings with Defoe.

In these ships [the Duke and Dutchess] Captain W Woodes Rogers also brought away Alexander Selkirk from Juan Fernandez, whose papers being put in the hands of Daniel Defoe were drawn out into the story of Robinson Crusoe.

(F Brown, *History and Antiquities of Nailsea Court,* 1876)

Mr Walter Wilson's opinion is that when Defoe was lodging at a public house in Castle Street, Bristol, he met with Capt. Rogers or Alexander Selkirk himself, and so got the frame-work of Robinson Crusoe.

(*Gloucestershire Notes and Queries,* 1881)

Damaris [Daniel] married three times, in each case to men of wealth and standing [...] When she was an old lady, living at 16 St James' Square, the widow of her third husband, Thomas Daniel, she often told how Defoe and Selkirk met at her house.

(SH Evans, *The Book of Nailsea Court*)

The question of whether or not Defoe and Selkirk ever met has been a big challenge for researchers for many years. The idea of the existence of Selkirk's 'papers' is surely quite electrifying and some convincing circumstantial evidence for both their existence and several Defoe and Selkirk meetings is offered by Mark Steeds, confident that he can support such evidence with some of the references he has found over the years, for example:

The present spot has further associations with the memories of Robinson Crusoe. Nearly opposite the north-east end of St Peter's Church [now just a shell after heavy bombing] is Cock and Bottle Lane, wherein stands the Star Inn, a tavern that in the last century was a sort of local Mitre to all the convivial wits of Bristol. This inn stands, or rather stood, for it has been lately altogether transformed, upon the site of the Northern Keep of the castle ... Our purpose in mentioning the inn, however, is to remark that among its guests in the early part of the last century was Daniel Defoe. He had fled from London to escape his creditors, and was known amongst his acquaintances in Bristol as the 'Sunday Gentleman', from the fact of his daring to appear in the streets only on that day. His biographer, Mr Wilson, states that a friend of his resident in the city relates, 'that one of his ancestors remembered Defoe, and sometimes saw him walking in the streets of Bristol, accoutred in the fashion of the times, with a fine flowing wig, lace ruffles and a sword by his side'. The same writer adds that 'one Mark Watkins who left the Red Lion in Castle Street, which Defoe also used to visit, was wont to entertain his company in after times with an account of a singular personage who made his appearance in Bristol, clothed in goat skins, in which dress he was in the habit of walking the streets, and went by the name of Alexander Selkirk or Robinson Crusoe'.

('Daniel Defoe and Robinson Crusoe', *Bristol Past and Present* Volume II, 1881)

And from *Life of Selkirk,* Isaac James, 1861:

To place, says Mr Harford, beyond the dispute of any 12 impartial persons the fact that Selkirk placed his papers in Defoe's hands, and that from them he wrote *Robinson Crusoe*, it was related by Mrs Daniel (a granddaughter of Major Wade, who was wounded in the battle of Sedgemoor) to Mr Joseph Harford, of Dighton Street, Bristol [...]

that 'she knew him well, and that he told her such was the case'.

All of this raises one intriguing question. Assuming that Selkirk's 'papers' did exist – as there are plenty of references to them – and that Defoe took them away to help in his *Crusoe* creation, he would surely have promised to return them; but it seems that he did not. It has to be said that, even then, even before he wrote his great classic, such notes must have been worth a pretty penny, for Selkirk was already famous through the Woodes Rogers book. And what form might they have taken? Were they loose or were they bound in a volume as a journal of the day would have been?

Whatever shape they took, it is possible to surmise that very few people knew of them or their contents apart from Selkirk, Defoe, the ultimate custodian and one other, who had obviously been acquainted with their existence by the marooned mariner himself.

That was his wife, Frances Candia or Candia, the buxom gold-digging landlady of his favourite pub in Plymouth where he was latterly based with the Royal Navy. She thought he was 'a worthless rogue' but, after he died aboard HMS *Weymouth* off Africa in 1721, she pursued his wealth and goods with dogged determination, brandishing the will he had rashly written in her favour, after also writing one favouring his first (common-law) wife, Sophia Bruce, the Largo lass he had earlier taken south with him and then neglected.

Not content with destroying Sophia's rights and trying to purloin her rings, Frances even went to Largo to claim Selkirk's property. But having thus gained riches beyond all her reasonable expectations, she still had her acquisitive eyes on a bigger prize.She had obviously heard a story (from

Selkirk himself?) that the Duke of Hamilton in Scotland was in possession of 'a journal' the sailor had kept while marooned, and doubtless realised just how sensational – and valuable – an acquisition that would be: the original diary of the original Robinson Crusoe! It was a credible scenario, considering how Defoe was always broke. During his time as an English spy in Scotland, he would surely have become known to the Duke of Hamilton, a prime mover in the Union debate – first resisting Scotland's merger with England and then accepting it.

Languishing in debt after the first flush of *Crusoe* success, did Defoe have reason to seek out a rich man, preferably a Scot, who might be interested in buying the papers of a famous fellow Scot? So, feigning poverty and grief, the widowed Frances wrote to the duke at Hamilton Palace in 1724, apparently in the hope of getting her hands on it.

She wrote in her petition:

To his Grace the Duke of Hamilton re:
The most humble Petition of Frances Selkirk...

That Yr Grace's Petitionr is the widdow of Alexander Sel-kirk who was left on the desolate island called Ferdinando where he continued alone four years and four months all which time he kept a journal of his observations as also of the Voyages he made with Capt. Dempiore as also in the Duke which took the Aquaperlea Ship in the South Sea which ship Yr Petitionr's husband had in his charge as Commander to bring to England and upon his arrival his late Grace Yr most noble Father then desireing to see the abovesaid journal of Petitionr's said Husband did leave it with him after which, proceeding again to leave on another voyage, died in the same.

To this day the successive dukes and their researchers have failed to find such a literary treasure in their grand library at Lennoxlove House near Edinburgh. Were the 'papers' and 'journal' one and the same thing? We will probably never know, as Frances did not get an answer from the Duke, and the current Duke of Hamilton has been unable to help find what, if they exist at all, must now be among the most valuable written documents on earth – whether they contributed minimally or greatly to the creation of *Robinson Crusoe*.

3

Brodie's Final Trick?

HE WAS TO become one of the most notorious criminals in the Scottish capital's long, often dark history. And when he was finally caught, William Brodie was especially reviled, not only because of his dastardly deeds but also because of his betrayal of his class. He was a 'respectable' businessman and town councillor (or Deacon) who would occasionally become a totally different person whose double life inspired his fellow Edinburgher Robert Louis Stevenson to create the world-famous story of Jekyll and Hyde. His errant behaviour and what he got up to at night was often characterised by mystery.

Indeed, when he began his 'other' nocturnal life, the city's citizenry were quite bewildered. Crimes kept happening that seemed to have been the work not of a common thief but of a ghost. For more often than not, entry to the affected premises seemed to have been achieved by the perpetrator walking though the walls, or at least through the locked doors. The wave of thefts began in mid-1786 and went like this:

12 August: The outer door of Messrs Johnston and Smith, bankers in the Royal Exchange, is opened and over £800 taken from the drawers.

9 October: The Parliament Close shop of goldsmith James Wemyss loses 50 gold and diamond rings, brooches and earrings, also a whole variety of valuable spoons.

12 November: Bridge Street hardware merchants McKain's has clearly been broken into – the lock that should have kept out intruders has been breached – 17 steel watch-chains missing.

8 December: The shop of John Law, tobacconist in the Exchange, is broken into and a canister containing between £10 and £12 carried off.

Christmas Eve: From their shop at the corner of Bridge Street and High Street – just opened, with a new door and lock fitted – a distressed John and Andrew Bruce report that several gold and silver watches and rings worth £350 have gone missing in the night.

Christmas Day: Goldsmith John Tapp is relieved of 18 guinea notes, a 20 shilling note, a silver watch and some valuable rings from his broken-into home, while being detained at his shop by a bottle-wielding customer on the pretext of having a merry seasonable drink.

August 1787: Grocer John Carnegie of Leith loses a huge quantity of fine black tea. Oddly, some of it is recovered when tea-packed parcels are found along the length of the road from Leith to Edinburgh. It is assumed the burglars found their weight too much to bear.

29 October: The burglars return to the heart of the city with a raid on a fashionable shoemaker's shop in Royal Exchange. Losses may have been light as they are not recorded.

30 October: The college mace – a three-century-old silver

masterpiece – goes missing from Edinburgh University library. An appeal goes out: 'A reward of ten guineas, to be paid by the City Chamberlain, is hereby offered for the discovery of all or any of the persons responsible.'

9 January 1788: The silk shop of Messrs Inglis and Horner loses £500 worth of satins and silks. The Procurator Fiscal puts up a £150 reward, and promises a free pardon for any accomplice turning king's evidence.

And so it goes on, until 5 March 1788, which proves to be a fateful date with destiny for the mysterious burglar and his gang; the night of the botched final job that starts the downfall of a man who thought he could cheat people, justice, and even death. The target is nothing less than Scotland's General Excise Office. Of which more later...

For William Brodie, the birth of Edinburgh's New Town in 1766, when he was a tender 25, meant a new surge of business. For anyone skilled in the making of furniture, what was to be a century-long development of classical homes on Edinburgh's northern fields marked a golden age of enviable prosperity. He was already feeling the benefits by sharing in his father Francis's growing workload when the old man died at 74 in 1780 – just as the plan to transform reekie old Edinburgh into the Athens of the North was getting into its elegant stride.

Waves of public and private money were being invested into the grand initiative of Provost George Drummond (little of which he would live to see) to attract not just the city's own professionals and aristocracy out of the overcrowded Old Town but expatriates 'of rank' who now saw, set against the claustrophobia of London, a breathable future amid the wide avenues and Doric, Ionic and Corinthian pillars of their own grand capital. Wealthy Scots riding a sudden wave of industrial enterprise in building, iron works, land ownership, law, banking, sugar and tobacco importation, brewing, publishing and commerce generally were gathering here to seek out new lives, new homes... and new furniture.

It meant that, on his father Francis's death, William Brodie's legacy was multi-faceted: the means through inherited ownership of the family business and property to exploit that great tide of money-making opportunity; a lump sum of £10,000; and – perhaps most significant of all – his father's spotless reputation as an upstanding citizen and councillor.

And the son who did not quite make it to the old widower's departure – who had been too busy sleeping off 'the night before' at a mistress's house – also received the benefit of any doubt. With his weaknesses and indiscretions not yet recognised by wider society, he was seen as a chip off the old master craftsman and gentleman, who had been Deacon of the Incorporation of Wrights, cabinet-maker extraordinary and Mason of Lodge Kilwinning, Canongate. Surely William would be another safe pair of Brodie hands? And so, within a year the bereaved son was filling his father's shoes as a Deacon Councillor of the City, a position that gave him primary access to lucrative council projects in his field. It seemed William Brodie had been left holding a whole handful of life's trump cards, which must have felt like quite a triumph for one so keen on gambling.

So how would he play it? The safest bet would be to feign a furrowed brow of grief and hold all these cards close to his chest while relaxing into his perceived respectability and watching his potential customer base grow organically. But if the truth were known, his wayward soul was not enamoured of safety or respectability. He was cunning enough to present that face to the world, but under the shadow of his three-cornered hat there was a mischievous and calculating brain that sought the darker side of life, drawn to illegitimate adventure.

Though he enjoyed the fruits of the New Town's demands, his life was intensely centred around the Old Town and he sensed that he would still thrive there, knowing that the privileged people in the newly-gentrified north still needed commercial premises catering for basic human needs; their architectural masterpiece boasted relatively few shops, workshops, pubs, hotels or clubs. So with little in the way of fine shopping, furnishings and social contact immediately to hand in their still-growing community, this higher society still saw the Old Town – before Princes Street emerged with luxury shops and products – as a place to revisit.

None of these cultural developments, prestigious buildings or changing circumstances would have been missed by the calculating 41-year-old Brodie, who was easily tempted by money-making opportunities, and who, as a breeder and owner of fighting cocks, could often be found at Henderson's Stables in the Grassmarket cheering on his own feathered champions. He also loved tavern card and dice games and, while often losing, would go to extraordinary lengths to win. In other words, he cheated. And with immediate financial concerns lifted from his shoulders he succumbed more than ever to the weaker side of his character and the recreational enjoyments of spending unwisely.

That included his two most expensive obligations, a pair of mistresses and their broods who required keeping in the manner to which they had become accustomed: Ann Grant, who lived near St James's Square with three children fathered by Brodie, and Jean Watt, who lived with two more of his children in Libberton's Wynd.

Despite his business going relatively well with his privileged access to civic work and high demand from wealthy private clients, it began to dawn on him that his after-hours lifestyle could not be maintained on what he could earn legally, even with the help of his fast-diminishing inheritance, and that something would inevitably have to give.

The process developed over some six years with other negatives – huge gaming debts, a taste for late-night drinking and out-of-bounds women – gathering to create the perfect financial storm. Though unable or unwilling to tame himself, he finally saw that his new life could only end one way, though his 'respectable' side could not abide the idea of bankruptcy. By 1786 he had decided a new tack was urgently needed, and it would have to be about generating 'enough' income.

This was the catalytic moment that marked the birth of Deacon Brodie's active criminal half.

In many ways his life had been already divided into two, as contrasting as night and day: the neat, tidy and superficially charming man who walked and talked his way around the city's daytime world of hearty greetings, respectful social contact, deals and dealmakers, and his opposing night-time world of flickering street lanterns, dark closes, drunken trysts, dubious motivations, violence and shady contacts.

Though it was at first a secret only to himself, this darker half that he feigned to struggle with but really relished, was about to take over his life. It had occurred to him during his legitimate work – the making of cabinets with doors and house or office doors themselves – that even if he had not fitted them himself, he had exclusive access to some clients' keys, having a whole selection either directly to hand or being able to find and copy them. And while the conclusion of this thought was forming, a double opportunity was presenting itself. The council had decided, with the inclusion of his vote, to clear away the ancient cobbles of the High Street and lower its overall level, with the attendant need to replace doors (often with new locks), which was, almost literally, just up Brodie's street. So many keys! So many chances to access other people's premises! It was more than such an easily tempted man could resist.

And so it all began, the long series of sinister house and shop break-ins that suddenly gripped the city centre and deeply puzzled it too, as some places were entered with so little or no disturbance and damage.

For Brodie the delicious irony of it all was that – while making all the right shocked noises to the victims and acquaintances about such 'outrageous' thefts – he himself was benefiting from shocked property owners asking for increased security in the form of stronger doors and better locks.

There were 11 break-ins in all, the first perpetrated by Brodie himself who, on such expeditions, carried a shaded lantern and dressed in a crêpe mask and dark clothes. He made his first mistake when he began to work with three dubious accomplices. First to be recruited – as a daytime locksmith for the Brodie workshop as well as on nocturnal projects – was a Berkshire refugee called George Smith, who had taken shelter at the Grassmarket stables of Michael Henderson, which housed not just horses and fighting cocks but (said one historian) 'the lower order of travellers'.

Being around there a lot to cheer on his own feathered friends, Brodie soon befriended Smith, having noted his dire circumstances and his skills as a locksmith. With his physical and financial health deteriorating fast, surely Smith would be open to 'ideas' to improve his lot? Brodie suggested 'something being done to advantage' – and did not have to ask twice. The 'doing of something' was clearly nothing new or daunting to Smith, who was quickly brought on board and just as quickly improved his lot by setting up home with a front as a small grocery shop in the Cowgate. He often went along with his boss to his favourite den of iniquity, Clark's gambling house in Fleshmarket Close, where, over well-lubricated card games, they both roped in two more recruits: Andrew Ainslie, sometime shoemaker in Edinburgh, and another Englishman-on-the-run, John Brown.

Two Scots and two Englishmen, stretching across several strata of society. But what they had in common was the fact that each was a misfit in one way or another. Such a motley little army needed a little general, and, after doing the first 'job' himself, Brodie began to revel in that role as project-planning became increasingly precise and sophisticated.

Until they got to the big-prize challenge… the Excise Office. Tackling that would be the most audacious criminal enterprise ever tried in Scotland: an attack on the very revenues of the nation. For this, Brodie wore a dark greatcoat, a black cocked hat and a black wig. He carried a dark lantern, a rope to tie up the old watchman, crepe masks for all four of them, a whistle for Ainslie to communicate 'danger' in codes, and a key that would fit the heavy main door.

How did he get his hands on that? Having once visited the Excise Office with a friend, Brodie had taken note of its layout and of course its endless store of good citizens' cash; he resolved to know it even better and on another visit with Smith saw the key of the outer door hanging on a nail. He had Smith create a diversion while he quickly produced a handful of putty to make an impression of it. The resulting replica was successfully tested on a trial break-in; but for the event itself several more tools were brought to hand, most notably a number of loaded pistols.

The acquiring of weak playmates – it would soon transpire – proved a big mistake in Brodie's criminal career. But acquiring guns was an even more reckless misjudgement, for their life-threatening potential could well have had a critical bearing on his own life. Burglary was one thing, the capacity to kill quite another, perhaps even enough to justify a sentence of death in those less-forgiving times. His shocked colleagues certainly recognised that. But did he?

As the nervous, odd little band made their heavily laden way down the Canongate towards Chessels Court at about 8pm, they could not have imagined just how badly wrong this final enterprise would go. Three factors would expose the sheer folly of it: the disappointment at their poor haul (about £16 when they expected £1,000); the resulting embitterment of Brown; and the surprise appearance of a late-working bank official. In a newspaper report telling the whole story, the key sentence was: 'Mr James Bonar of the Excise Office discovered the criminals in the very act of theft.'

The gang scattered and made off at speed, but it was soon clear they were reaching the end of the road. When they gathered at Smith's house the next day the others were unimpressed by Brodie's excuses and promises of better projects in the pipeline, and Brown was waiting only to collect his £4 share of the Excise Office loot before making his way to the Sheriff-Clerk's office to reveal all and start to plea-bargain. He would take the law officials up to the foot of Salisbury Crags at dead of night and show them, under a lifted stone, the gang's stash of false keys. He would also reveal the names of his accomplices (but not yet Brodie's) so that the fiscal ordered the sheriff-clerk to 'make the necessary arrangements to apprehend our friend's companions, Ainslie and Smith'. For some reason – leaving open the option of blackmail? – Brown initially kept his powder dry on the naming and shaming of the kingpin.

It was when Brodie himself tried to visit them in jail, perhaps to get a hint on whether his name had been mentioned, that he began to sense that it had. What he didn't yet know was that, as well as Brown and Ainslie, Smith had come clean and confessed to the robbery of the college mace, of Tapp's home, of a tea shop in Leith and also of the Inglis and Horner shop. Smith also disclosed the extensive robbery of the Bruces' shop and revealed that Brodie had been a key participant in almost all the crimes.

Though not yet in possession of such facts, Brodie sensed the game was well and truly up, and within hours, on Sunday 9 March 1788, when most good people were in church, he was in a post chaise clattering away off down the Canongate, past the pleasure garden of Comely Green, and charging through East Lothian on his way south.

Where was he fleeing to? For a fare-and-accommodation outlay of five guineas, he was hoping to reach London via Dunbar, Newcastle and York on the first stage of a new life. The authorities so much wanted to know his destination that they issued this urgent notice:

TWO HUNDRED POUNDS OF REWARD

Whereas WILLIAM BRODIE, a considerable house carpenter and burgess of the city of Edinburgh, has been charged with being concerned in breaking into the General Excise Office for Scotland, and stealing from the Cashier's office there a sum of money – and as the said William Brodie has either made his escape from Edinburgh, or is still concealed about that place – a REWARD of ONE HUNDRED AND FIFTY POUNDS STERLING is hereby offered to any person who will produce him alive at the Sheriff Clerk's Office, Edinburgh, or will secure him, so that he may be brought there within a month from this date; and FIFTY POUNDS STERLING MORE payable upon his conviction, by William Scott, procurator fiscal for the shire of Edinburgh.

So began the second 'mystery' period of Deacon Brodie's life. Where on earth was he heading to get himself lost? According to a later-disclosed letter to his brother-in-law, his intention was to reach New York where an American clergyman, primed by a Scottish colleague, would gather him up and, presumably, help him to repent. The letter ended: 'Let my name and destination be a profound secret for fear of bad consequences.'

From London, where he realised the Bow Street Runners had been alerted to hunt him down, he made his getaway by boat from Blackwall across the North Sea to Ostend. But even there the net was closing as, unknown to him, a British consul-appointed amateur detective (Irishman John Daly) was soon hard on his trail. He followed that trail to Amsterdam where the Scot was confident of finding to a berth on a weapon-laden vessel servicing the last skirmishes of America's independence conflict.

But it was not to be. He would never reach even the coast of Holland far less the harbour of New York. Daly tracked him down to the little room where he was living – under the name of John Dixon – above a pub called the Lommer crouched in an alley called Zoutsteeg, just off the boat-busy central artery of the Damrak. Having surely thought he was nearly home and dry, it must have been a stunning shock for Brodie to hear the repeated knocking on his door. Getting no answer, Daly burst through it, opened the cupboard in which Brodie was cowering, and formally arrested him. 'How do you do, Captain John Dixon alias William Brodie!' the big man boomed. 'I must ask you to come along with me.'

The fugitive went quietly, allowing himself a deep sigh of disappointment as he gathered together what clothes he could, before being hustled down the stairs past an astonished landlord.

Even before he was marched the two hundred metres to his holding cell below the Dam Square townhouse, it was clear that the ever-clever William Brodie, still with an enigmatic smirk on the edge of his mouth, was never going to lose faith in his own survivability.

Not even when, after his heavily-escorted return to Edinburgh he was sentenced to death at his trial there in late August 1788. Not even when they put a noose around his neck on the first day of the following October… which brings us to the final Brodie mystery. The truths, half-truths and outright fabrications that persist today regarding his dramatic demise had begun to take root even before he stepped up to the gallows. He was already a less-than-admired legend in his lifetime, though that life was about to be cut short at the age of 47. Or was it? Feeding the many stories about the end, or not, of this diminutive but larger-than-life character was his strangely relaxed and almost arrogant attitude towards the final curtain. A huge crowd of around 40,000 had gathered to witness the spectacle before his jailhouse, the dilapidated 14th century Old Tolbooth, a stone's throw from his Lawnmarket workshop and home; to many of them something about his easy demeanour suggested he did not believe the curtain was really going to fall. Perhaps it was just his final defence mechanism, a what-the-hell denial in the face of such a momentous prospect or – more likely – there was something more complex and cunning going on inside the scheming brain of this man who had always believed he was one of life's survivors.

One of death's survivors too? Could he really cheat the hangman's rope? The most common scandalous tale that has lived on was that he engaged a surgeon to fashion a steel tube to fit inside or – more likely – around his throat and protect it from the squeezing of the rope during the 'fatal' drop, and that the executioner had been bribed not to notice the odd bulge around his neck. Indeed, the Deacon was seen to converse with the hangman several times at the scaffold while having the rope's length adjusted, this apparently with a professional eye, as the skilled cabinet-maker was said to have been involved in the previous year's redesign of the awful apparatus – irony of ironies, if true!

Even if Brodie's part in the death-dealing redesign was only partial, he was certainly familiar with the new gallows and some suspected he knew how to manipulate its workings to his advantage. Would that explain the condemned man's quiet confidence in the face of his impending doom? What was going on?

Another persistent story was that he had made an arrangement with an Edinburgh-resident French doctor, Pierre de Gravers, after a 'consultation' with him in his Old Tolbooth cell as his date with destiny drew close. And if Brodie's life prospects were looking pretty grim, his living conditions were even grimmer; so it would have surprised few if intolerance of his rat-infested existence had moved him to a last request for treatment for depression.

But in the 34 days between his trial beginning in late August 1788 and his early October rendezvous with the scaffold, he somehow managed to keep up his spirits by dressing well despite being in chains, singing extracts from *The Beggar's Opera* and playing draughts with himself and any interested visitors. He was allowed a longer chain than was normal, as well as pen and ink, and occasional visits from friends.

Many such prisoners would be held here before being executed or, if lucky, transported off to work on the American plantations. And by the time Brodie was ready to get as far away as possible from the scaffold, the now-independent Americans had closed the door – though a new one had opened at Australia's Botany Bay. With that escape route in mind, the Deacon had another couple of cards up his sleeve. With only two weeks left to live, officially, he appealed to a pair of VIPs in the vain hope that their influence could, even at that late stage, change the course of his court-decided fate. Datelined the Tolbooth, 10 September 1788, the first letter was to the Right Hon Henry Dundas (Viscount Melville) and part of it read:

I most humbly beseech your interposition and interest in support of this application making in London in my be-half and if possible prevent me from suffering an Ignom-nious Death to the disgrace of my numerous conections, even if it were to end my days at Bottony Bay.

The second letter, with the same dateline, was to Her Grace the Duchess of Buccleuch, and read in part:

With all the fortitude of a man, I must confess to you,

Madam, that I feel the Natural horror at Death, and particularly a violent Ignominious Death, and would willingly avoid it even on the condition of spending my Future years at Bottony Bay.

What, then, of the good French doctor? His visit to this forbidding place – if it happened at all – was said to have concerned more body than mind or soul. It was suspected that he had undertaken, presumably for a good price, to revive Brodie after his body's release from the rope and that, to effect helpful bleeding, he had pencil-marked the condemned man's arms and temples to indicate where he would make the cuts.

It is tempting to conclude that Brodie's defiantly relaxed manner on the scaffold had something to do with such an apparently reassuring strategy, though his unexpected behaviour at that critical point may also have reflected his perverse enjoyment of the limelight after all these dark days lurking and hiding from people down damp, pitch-black closes. But where was his big farewell speech to the thousands of onlookers? Such an egotist would surely have wanted to speak out boldly (yet humbly) in his own defence and take his leave with something of a swagger. The absence of such a piece of theatre seemed to confirm that he intended to return from his appointment with the Grim Reaper.

To friends he had seen more privately that morning, he had seemed remarkably self-possessed, cool, contained and almost indifferent to his fate, speaking of it light-heartedly as 'a leap in the dark'. He had shown real emotion only when visited, for the last time, by his pretty ten-year-old daughter Cecil, 'and here nature and the feelings of a father were superior to every other consideration; and the falling tear which he endeavoured to suppress gave strong proofs of his sensibility – he embraced her with emotion and blessed her with the warmest affection'. That observation was courtesy of *The Scots Magazine,* which further reported:

When Mr Brodie came to the scaffold, he bowed politely to the magistrates and the people. He had on a full suit of black – his hair dressed and powdered. Smith was dressed in white linen, trimmed with black. Having spent some time in prayer, with seeming fervency, with the clergymen, Mr Brodie then prayed a short time by himself.

Having put on white nightcaps, Brodie pointed to Smith to ascend the steps that led to the drop, and, in an easy manner, clapping him on the shoulder, said: 'George Smith, you are first in hand.' Upon this, Smith, whose behaviour was highly penitent and resigned, slowly ascended the steps and was immediately followed by Brodie, who mounted with briskness and agility, and examined the dreadful apparatus with attention, and particularly the halter designed for himself. The ropes being too short-tied, Brodie stepped down to the platform and entered into conversation with his friends. He then sprang up again but the rope was still too short; and he once more descended to the platform showing some impatience.

During this dreadful interval Smith remained on the drop with great composure and placidness. Brodie having ascended a third time, and the rope being at last properly adjusted, he deliberately untied his neckcloth, buttoned up his waistcoat and coat, and helped the executioner to fix the rope. He then pulled the nightcap over his face and placed himself in an attitude expressive of firmness and resolution.

Smith, who during all this time had been in fervent devotion, let fall a handkerchief as a signal, and a few minutes before three they were launched into eternity, almost without a struggle.

This execution was conducted with more than usual solemnity; and the great bell tolled during the ceremony, which had an awful and solemn effect. The crowd of spectators was immense.

Some aspects of the whole affair were so murky it was hardly surprising that conspiracy stories kept emerging and circulating – such as the widespread suspicion that the hangman had been bargained with to arrange for a short fall, thus the inordinate time spent fiddling with the rope. The following elaboration is from Robert Chambers' *Traditions of Edinburgh:*

His dress and deportment at the gallows displayed a mind at ease, and gave some countenance to the popular notion that he had made certain mechanical arrangements for saving his life...When placed on that insecure pedestal, and while the rope was adjusted around his neck by the executioner, his courage did not forsake him. On the contrary, even there he exhibited a sort of levity; he shuffled about, looked gaily around, and finally went out of the world with his hand stuck carelessly into the open front of his vest.

Or did he? William Roughead, the Scottish lawyer, editor and essayist, wrote in his *Classic Crimes,* after much research, that an early plan to rescue the Deacon – by overpowering the city and guard and breaking into the Tolbooth – had been abandoned by his friends in favour of a more sophisticated strategy; this was the one that now (allegedly) went into operation. When cut down, Brodie's body was handed over to two of his own workmen, who quickly placed it on a cart, and drove it at a full, bone-shaking pace round the back of the castle, presumably with the idea that such a rough ride might provoke resuscitation. That was not to be, but the corpse was then taken to one of Brodie's workshops in the Lawnmarket, where Dr de Gravers was reportedly in attendance. However, all attempts at bleeding failed; Brodie had not been breathing for many long minutes and was finally pronounced to be 'fairly gone'. Another report said:

> After the Magistrates retired a vein was opened. It is said other means of recovery were used after the body was taken away, but the neck was found to be dislocated.

All of which would sound decidedly terminal to any sensible person, so why – even when Brodie had (apparently) found his way to an unmarked grave at the Buccleuch Church in Chapel Street – was his demise not accepted by so many? There was widespread local talk that, after a set-up exit, a 'born-again' Brodie had found his way abroad. Some said he had fled to his original escape destination of New York; others swore he had been seen on the streets of Paris where he had taken up residence. *Pardon?* as they might say in the French capital. Roughead again: 'There is a tradition that, on a subsequent occasion, the grave was opened, when no trace of his body could be found.'

The theories still bubble on, well into the third century of Deacon Brodie's dark story, but there is little chance of doubts being settled now, as the burial ground is now covered by a car park behind university lecture halls.

But just for the fascination of it, let's think about this more than one-dimensionally. 'The neck was found to be dislocated' – who said that? If it is to be attributed to Dr de Gravers, who would have been part of any getaway conspiracy, it is not a huge stretch of the imagination to respond, 'He would say that, wouldn't he?' It's what Edinburgh University's Owen Dudley Edwards calls his 'Mandy Rice Davies theory' (look it up) and, as one who has written and broadcast many thousands of words on the Brodie case, he feels there are many other areas of doubt about the 'death' that have never really been resolved.

The historian and author of many academic books leans towards the theory that Brodie was revived and removed from the scene of his 'death'. While conceding that there is no solid evidence, he feels that the middle-class miscreant 'was so well-connected in Edinburgh society that his fate would have been comprehensively protected by them when any official or reporter asked them or his doctor for confirmation of his demise'. In other words, the enquirers would have been sold a dummy or, to put it bluntly, told an outright lie.

'Let's face it,' says the historian, 'this could have been the idea from the start – for the cheating of the gallows to succeed, for friends to be primed to say he was gone, to feign grief, see off any questioners and, once the episode had blown over, to quietly help him out of the city and the country.'

Dudley Edwards thinks it likely that Brodie was hidden away for a while, provided with new identity and disguise, and 'smuggled to America' where he lived out his days. He argued with persuasive conviction in a feature called *Case Reopened* on BBC Radio Scotland:

Brodie's excellent connections stretched to the judge himself at the trial, who was embarrassed he had known Brodie and, more importantly, 'kent his fether'. And let's not forget what a clever man this uncommon thief was. He would not have given up his life easily, that's for sure, and would have employed every possible means at his disposal to sustain it. So I believe it's more than possible that he survived. The only evidence we have that he died are the statements to that effect from the people around him, but these were his own friends. They said he was dead but, frankly, that was not reliable evidence. You wouldn't expect them to say anything else. We know his friends put out a very odd story, that he had hoped to survive, but had failed. So basically, it was all very suspicious. It suggests they were anxious to prevent rumours that this is exactly what had happened...

Whether or not he was hanged on a gibbet of his own design, he had been certainly involved to some degree of consultancy on its reconception the year before, so he understood the new workings. He knew he ran the risk of being hanged and knew how he could have a good chance of avoiding it. The gibbet was reinforced so that it didn't break his neck on the first drop...

And if the rope was the right length he would be okay. There would have been a bit of a jar, but he had a plan and nothing would have been broken. Once supposedly hanged, he would plunge through a platform taking him out of sight. The structure underneath the actual gallows was hidden away from the public. And Brodie's friends were there, immediately receiving the body, and he was almost certainly still alive. He would have been taken down very quickly and spirited away.

So resurrection is a distinct probability? 'It is at least as good a theory as any other, and I would say a good deal better,' says Dudley Edwards with a mischievous twinkle.

Which prompts the listener to suspect he would find it rather a shame if the mystery were ever to be solved.

4

What Lies Beneath?

YOU HAVE TO wear a builder's hard-hat before descending the modern set of steel steps that take you 14 feet down into the trembling chill of this ancient labyrinth of little caves, passages, seating areas, and chambers, all hand-carved out of sandstone. Not because it's really dangerous, but because if you are taller than the people who built it, you are liable to hit your head on the ceiling.

It is said, of course, that people were much smaller in those days; and by sensing the closeness of that ceiling (which occasionally does hit your hat), you have to conclude that 'those days' must have been long ago indeed. And much longer, no doubt, than the time of local blacksmith George Paterson who claimed to have created the Gilmerton Cove in the 1720s.

The whole maze-like thing must add up to a quarter-mile of pillars and recesses, which, he said, he had hollowed from solid sandstone with a pick-axe in five years, before using it to accommodate his working smithy, his family of wife and three sons, and his booze collection, which got him into serious trouble with the Kirk a few years later.

It must be said here that 'drinking den for local gentry' is one of the many suggestions put forward – by expert and layman alike – to explain the presence of this rather sinister little cave system that lies below a betting shop and an innocent-looking white, pantiled cottage in traffic-packed Drum Street on Edinburgh's south side. Other suggested reasons for its existence, apart from the blacksmith's workshop, include illegal whisky still, smugglers' den, Masonic lodge, meeting place for persecuted religious groups, witches' coven, Knights Templar hideout, abandoned mine, Covenanters' church, tomb of an ancient king, and even the home of the notorious 18th-century Hellfire Club ('for people of quality involved in debased religious practices').

Indeed, just to confuse matters, the 2007 television documentary series *Cities of the Underworld* suggested Gilmerton Cove was linked to a nearby Hellfire Club building by a secret passage.

None of which supports Mr Paterson's story, equally dodgy in its own way, especially when you realise – on viewing the place – the utter impossibility of one man hacking it out with chisels, even in 20 years, even with dozens of helpers. Then add the blacksmith's forge that has clearly never been used; the well that doesn't reach down to the water table; the fireplace without a chimney and no signs of having held anything hot; not to mention the rock-solid seating areas and tables carved out at every opportunity as if in expectation of many guests.

On one of those tables there is not only a gouged-out 'punch bowl' (maybe) but some ancient-looking graffiti that pictures a cat (maybe) and a date of 1099 (maybe). And if there is some doubt about their legibility they seem to carry more credibility as clues to the real origins of the place than the blacksmith's claim that was once swallowed whole – in the early 1800s when a guidebook by D Webster asserted that the Cove was 'very popular among people of fashion from Edinburgh'.

Its appeal faded in the next two centuries; but the Cove's tour guide, Margaretanne Dugan, saw it reopen as an educational resource for the community as well as a tourist attraction in 2010, backed by a modern reception area, display cases, and website that now pulls in – by appointment – scores of visitors mainly from abroad.

Despite her longish career with the attraction, which is run by Gilmerton Heritage Trust along with City of Edinburgh Council, Ms Dugan is no nearer to finding an answer to the question of its original function than such first-time visitors are; though she does lean towards that '1099' date, personally believing that the place is liable to be about 1,000 years old.

That is an opinion partly shared by the prominent art expert and historian Julian Spalding, former head of Glasgow's museums and galleries, who goes one (millennium) better than the manager, believing the subterranean site is likely to have been a Druid temple dating back more than 2,000 years. He reckons it was deliberately buried by the ancient priests to protect its sacred nature, so that the effort pursued by blacksmith Paterson was probably more a digging-out-the-rubble exercise than a carving-out-from-scratch one.

The blacksmith's story was first challenged by FR Coles, assistant keeper of the National Museum of Antiquities in Edinburgh, writing in *The Scotsman* in 1897. Having made a detailed study of the caves, he reported that no one man could have carried out all this work in just a few years and he believed that the tool marks on every inch of the walls had been made by pointed objects and not by chisels (or pick-axes?). He concluded that the caves went back to a time much earlier than 18th century. And 120 years later it was the same newspaper that published Spalding's assertive new view:

It is very probable that the whole complex was deliberate-ly buried, a widespread ancient practice which prevented the subsequent defilement of sacred sites. This interpretation explains why two passages are still blocked by unexcavated rubble. It is inexplicable why Paterson should have filled them up after going to the immense trouble of excavating them.

Spalding believes the site could date back to the Iron Age and is of huge international significance because it is in such good condition:

The work is beautifully consistent throughout and indicates a team of highly-skilled craftsmen, with numerous assistants, guided by a mastermind. The arrangement of rooms and passages is elaborate and the dividing walls are often remarkably thin. All the shapes in the Cove are womb-like and curved, indicating a Celtic or earlier culture. The identification of Gilmerton Cove as a Druid temple makes sense of all the evidence. Druids were known to meet in secret in woods and caves away from habitation. Gilmerton is on a high ridge, marked with megaliths, overlooking Cramond, the site of mankind's earliest settlement in Scotland, and, later, a Roman Fort. If it is a Druid temple, discovered by chance in the 18th century, it will be the first substantial archaeological evidence of this sophisticated and highly-secretive priesthood.

All of which sounds quite compelling, and certainly more intriguing than the blacksmith's family home legend. But, while not denying that that could well have been its adopted function, the flow of grander theories about the Cove's original concept and purpose refuses to lie down and die. Speaking in a reception area festooned with posters of related ideas,

Ms Dugan adds one more – could it have been dedicated to Mithra, the ancient Iranian sun god whose worship permeated the Roman Empire and extended from India to Scotland? These days the ideas come from all over the globe. For example, Tomas McRae of Brisbane, Australia, writing in *Philalethes Magazine* after visiting the place that his Scots father had known:

> My late father, who visited The Cove as a child, told of exiting into an open field via one of the passages… How do I think it all began? Coal-mining is recorded at Gilmerton in 15th century or even earlier and limestone had also been mined there for centuries. The marks of pointed implements on the cave walls and furniture indicate that tools such as miners' picks were used to carve things to shape. A team of local miners must therefore be our prime suspects; but why dig it all out in the first place?

He goes on to suggest that when invading English troops passed through Gilmerton *en route* to Edinburgh, the cave system might have been created as a refuge:

> Rape, devastation, and pillage were the norm in those days and I believe the Cove started as a safe shelter for local residents when those forces threatened… It might have commenced with test digs for coal then later emergencies prompted this expansion… Local Presbyterian miners possibly used it as a church during their long persecution, carving the so-called punch bowl for a baptismal font. Years passed then an enterprising blacksmith took the place over as home and grog shop and the current legend began.

As if all of this intellectual puzzlement is not enough, the Cove has one more surprise up its sleeve. In the good old Edinburgh tradition, it could be haunted, suggests the manager. Why does she think that?

> One of our trustees asked the question 'What lies beyond the rubble in this room?', and I kid you not... when we played back the recording you could hear a voice saying [*whispers*] 'Never mind'.

Haunted or not... whatever it was or is, Gilmerton Cove has turned this Edinburgh suburb into a must-go-to spot on the city's heritage tourist trail, proving to be one of the most highly rated attractions since it reopened after a second modern reboot in 2010. 'The others don't have a ghost of a chance,' laughs Ms Dugan.

5

The Unkept Light

Though three men dwell on Flannan Isle
To keep the lamp alight
As we steered under the lexe we caught
No glimmer through the night

A passing ship at dawn had brought
The news, and quickly we set sail,
To find out what strange things might ail
The keepers of the deep-sea light

(Wilfrid Wilson Gibson)

THE FIRST PERSON to notice something wrong was the lookout on the passing tramp steamer *Archtor,* from Philadelphia. Reasonably certain of his ship's position just before midnight on 15 December 1900, he peered through the sea-fog expecting to see the two brilliant short flashes every 30 seconds that came from the Flannan Light. Normally they could be seen from a distance of 24 miles, and his ship was less than six miles away. But try as he might, he could not see the slightest flicker. All remained ominously dark and, although he did not then realise the significance of what he was reporting to his captain, that vaguely worrying revelation was to mark the beginning of one of the sea's most enduring mysteries.

Neither did the crew of the *Archtor,* steaming in such proximity to the remote lighthouse, realise just how near they were to solving the mystery there and then. For it was later established that whatever happened on that storm-beaten rocky islet, happened earlier that day. Had their curiosity been sufficiently aroused, they might have drawn closer, might even have attempted a landing, and might have discovered the true facts behind the riddle of the unkept light. In the absence of any immediate eye-witness evidence, however, the mystery has since given rise to much fantastic theorising and confounded not only succeeding generations of experts but also the thousands of ordinary people all over the world who have been intrigued by Wilfrid Wilson Gibson's epic poem on the tragic affair, written – largely from the imagination – 12 years after it happened.

What happened? That has always been, and remains, the question. The mystery is on a par with that of the *Mary Celeste* and bears a shadowy resemblance to it; for the three keepers who should have been tending the light on Eilean Mòr – one of the larger of the seven Flannan Islands, 18 miles north-west of the Outer Hebridean island of Lewis – simply vanished, leaving only the most minimal of clues to their fate. They could not have left by boat, for they did not have one. And when crew of the relief tender *Hesperus* arrived there some 11 days later, the first man ashore found only, in the words of Gibson's poem, 'a door ajar and an untouched meal and an overtoppled chair'.

It was an unmitigated shock to them, for – having left Oban just before the *Archtor* men put in there to report their non-sighting of the light – the *Hesperus* crew had been unaware, as they battled through a fierce gale towards the far-off archipelago, that there was anything amiss at all. As far as they were concerned, this was just a normal relief operation. But when they finally came within sight of the stubby 75-feet-tall tower, standing 330 feet high on the topmost point of Eilean Mòr, the absence of the usual welcoming flag was the first indication that all was not well. It was about noon on Boxing Day. The ship's captain, James Harvie, ordered that the steam whistle and siren be blasted twice, but there was no response from the blank windows. And a rocket fired from the ship, still so much under the weather that it could not safely release a landing boat, also died without an answer. With mounting alarm, Captain Harvie adjusted his telescope to scan the lighthouse anxiously... its squat outbuilding... the deserted plateau of the island... then the long stone stairway which connected these, down an almost sheer cliffside, to the crashing spray of the sea. With the exception of fluttering sea-birds, he saw absolutely no sign of life. 'Something's wrong!' he shouted, then ordered the boat out despite the bad weather.

As the sea heaved and buffeted the tiny vessel against the western landing stage, the relieving keeper, Joseph Moore, eventually managed to jump ashore to investigate. Clearly a brave man, he was nevertheless to be extremely traumatised by what he was to experience on the island; so much so that his superintendent, Robert Muirhead, would later write that 'if this nervousness does not leave Moore, he will require to be transferred'.

As he climbed the awesome, snakelike flight of 160 steps up the 200-foot cliffside, Moore called out the names of the colleagues he hoped to find at the top – James Ducat, Thomas Marshall and Donald McArthur – but all he received in reply were the shrieking cries of wheeling gulls and petrels. 'I went up and, on coming to the entrance gate,' he later wrote, 'I found it closed. I made for the door leading to the kitchen and storeroom. I found it closed. The door inside that was also closed, but the kitchen door itself was open.'

When he went into the kitchen Moore was surprised to find the table set as if a meal was about to begin. Apart from the overtoppled chair, everything seemed relatively normal, though the room had obviously been deserted for... how long? The clocks had stopped. 'I looked at the fireplace and saw that the fire was not lighted for some days. I entered the rooms in succession and found the beds empty, just as they left them in the early morning. I did not take time to search further, for I naturally well knew that something serious had occurred. I darted outside and made for the landing...'

There, he dramatically announced his fears to the waiting boatmen and persuaded two of them to join him in a more thorough investigation. They went back up with him to discover that 'unfortunately, my first impression was only too true'. Everything was in good order. Blinds were on the windows, pots and pans had been cleaned, the kitchen tidied up; and, on the professional side, the lamp had been trimmed, the oil fountains and canteens had been filled up, and the lens and machinery cleaned. It all seemed surprisingly correct, apart from the baffling fact that the keepers were not there.

Bewildered as he was, Moore still had a job to do. Once he had reported back to the *Hesperus,* he was given the help of two other seamen to man the light – and they soon had it back to work. 'We proceeded up to the light room and lighted the light at the proper time that night, and every night since.' That done, over the next two days, they continued the search for the missing men but, despite 'traversing the island from end to end, there was still nothing to convince us how it happened'.

Meanwhile, the *Hesperus* had made haste to Lewis to wire the news of the disaster to the Secretary of the Northern Lighthouse Board. And at 8.45 on that first night, an unhappily-disturbed Mr William Murdoch opened the door of his villa in

a gaslit street in Trinity, Edinburgh, to receive the following
message from a telegram boy:

> A dreadful accident has happened at Flannans. The three
> keepers, Ducat, Marshall and the Occasional, have dis-
> appeared from the island. On our arrival there this after-
> noon no sign of life was to be seen on the island. Fired
> rocket, but, as no response was made, managed to land
> Moore who went up to the station but found no keepers
> there. The clocks were stopped and other signs indicated
> that the accident must have happened about a week ago.
> Poor fellows, they must have been blown over the cliffs
> or drowned trying to secure a crane or something like that.
> Night coming on, we could not wait to make further in-
> vestigation, but will go off again to tomorrow morning to
> try and learn something as to their fate. I have left Moore,
> MacDonald, buoymaster, and two seamen on the island to
> keep the light burning until you make other arrangements.
> Will not return to Oban until I hear from you. I have re-
> peated this wire to [Northern Lighthouse Board Superin-
> tendent Robert] Muirhead, in case you are not at home. I
> will remain at the telegraph office tonight until it closes, if
> you wish to wire me. Master, *Hesperus*.

Captain Harvie's instant speculation on the cause of the
lightkeepers' disappearance has to take its place among a
plethora of ideas put forward over the years to explain the
tragedy, and prominent among these has to be Superintendent
Muirhead's. He was not only the last man to visit the
lightkeepers alive but also went to the island to officially
investigate the tragedy a few days after its discovery.

But to appreciate the various theories, one has to understand the shape and topography of Eilean Mòr. It is like a dog's head with the mouth on the right. The lighthouse is located in its eye socket, the east landing is under its chin, and the west landing up a high-sided, wave-lashed creek where a collar would be. A 400-yard incline rises from the west landing to the light.

In his report to the Commissioners of Northern Lighthouses, Muirhead pointed out that the last entry on 'the slate' (where notes were chalked before logging) had been made by Mr Ducat, the principal keeper, on the morning of 15 December. And as the *Archtor* had not seen the light that evening, it could be assumed that the men had disappeared between the last entry on the slate and the time they should have ignited the light that afternoon. The *Archtor* had also reported 'a very heavy sea' in the area later that day. Muirhead therefore focused on the possibilities of the men being washed or blown away while working together on an emergency either outside the lighthouse or at one of the landing stages. Finding no evidence of disturbance at the light or the east landing but finding some at the west – displaced railings, a dislodged stone block, and an unfastened lifebuoy – he came to the conclusion that it was there, at the west landing, that the men had met their fate. He wrote:

After a careful examination of the place, the railings, ropes etc., and weighing all the evidence which I could secure, I am of the opinion that the most likely explanation of the disappearance of the men is that they had all gone down on the afternoon [...] to the proximity of the West landing, to secure the box with the mooring ropes etc., and that an unexpectedly large roller had come up on the Island, and a large body of water going up higher than where they

were, and coming down upon them, had swept them away
with resistless force. I have considered the possibility of
the men being blown away by the wind, but, as the wind
was westerly, I am of the opinion, notwithstanding its
great force, that the more probable explanation is that they
have been washed away as, had the wind caught them, it
would, from its direction, have blown them up the Island
and I feel certain that they would have managed to throw
themselves down before they had reached the summit or
brow of the Island.

There are, however, certain nagging weaknesses about this
conclusion. Both the senior men's oilskins had been taken
from the station, as if they had gone out with some purpose and
plan. But, considering the rule that a lighthouse should not be
left unmanned, all three men would not be out at the same time
unless the last man were called to some dire emergency. But
if such an emergency had indeed been discovered at the west
landing, how could the last man, occasional keeper Donald
McArthur, have been summoned to it? Neither visual signal
nor cried-out sound would have reached him: the west landing
was too far away and obscured from sight. Yet the facts that
the kitchen chair was toppled and that McArthur's coat and
wellingtons were left behind suggest that he did indeed make
a dash outdoors, in his shirt-sleeves, into a freezing December
day. But if he was in such a hurry, why did he then bother to
shut doors and gates behind him?

It seems equally possible to surmise that a wave blown
from the west could have thrown the men upwards and
onto the incline above the cliffside, draining away to leave
them high if not dry – which is not to say that any of the
other theories is much more plausible. Some of the more

superstitious Hebridean islanders contend that the keepers were whisked from their rocky outpost by sea monsters. Others blame pirates, and perhaps the most outlandish idea is that they were abducted by giant sea-birds; this doubtless inspired the 'reincarnation' suggestion in Gibson's poem, which alludes to 'three queer black ugly birds... like seamen sitting bolt upright upon a half-tide reef'.

No belief has seemed too bizarre to explain the inexplicable. What about the spirit in St Flannan's Chapel, the sixth-century ruin that shares the bare plateau of Eilean Mòr with the lighthouse? Surely it had been offended by the inauguration, exactly one year before, of the intrusive light-flashing monument to modern man's lack of respect for the island's sacred peace? Surely it had simply taken its revenge.

Then there was the murder theory. Boredom and contempt-breeding familiarity had driven the men to hatred of each other. Cooped up in a small space with a wild, imprisoning sea all around them, it was only a matter of time before one of them cracked. And when that happened, he would have gone wild with violence, fighting the other two men into the sea just outside the lighthouse, then jumping in after them himself in a fit of remorse. Some credence can perhaps be accorded to this speculation by the fact that the bodies were never recovered. Had such an incident indeed occurred at the lighthouse are with the prevailing wind direction, the bodies would have been swept far out to sea; whereas drowning at the lower end of the island would probably have seen them washed up against the cliffs there.

Donald Macleod, one of the last keepers to live and work on Flannan before the light went automatic in 1971, was sure something like the struggle described above must have happened near the light station itself:

My theory is that one of the men went berserk. One of the others tried to calm him, but found this impossible and called for help. As the third keeper ran out of the kitchen to separate his colleagues, he knocked over the chair in his haste. Then the three struggled and fell to their death.

But another former keeper of the light – Walter Aldebert, who was there from 1953 to 1957 – preferred another story, which he painstakingly reconstructed after long hours photographically recording the frequency and height of occasional gigantic waves at the west landing. Such freak waves have always been a hazard at this point, particularly after severe storms. The west landing is in a narrow inlet ending in a cave and, when wave after wave is thundering through it, a high pressure of resident air can build up in the cave until it eventually explodes and sends tons of water washing over the cliffs. Mr Aldebert risked his life here many times to prove his conclusions which are now lodged as a report, unofficial and personal, with the Northern Lighthouse commissioners:

A storm is raging and Ducat is worried about his landing ropes. Nobody goes out of a lighthouse in bad weather, but if he loses his ropes, relief may be impossible, and he must save them if he can. After the wind starts to drop … leaving the cook… he and the other man put on their sea boots and coats and make their way to the west side. They come to the safety path which has a hand-rail, reaching the path which runs at right angles to the stairway and, seeing the path dry, they continue towards the crane where the box for stowing the landing ropes is situated. Suddenly a wave much bigger than the previous ones comes in and sweeps one of the men into the sea.

In a panic, the survivor races back to the light station for the third man – who knocks his chair from under him as he rushes out to help.

Grabbing a heaving line, the two men make their way back to the west side, hoping to throw the line to their unfortunate colleague. Then comes another huge wave, sweeping both men into the sea.

Despite Mr Aldebert's assiduous work on this theory, it is not easily accepted. Although such explosive waves can occasionally reach as high as 200 feet, and even the lamphouse can be splashed with spray at over 300 feet, a wave of 100 feet – the height required to reach the men and their work platform – would be a relative rarity, and two coming in such quick succession would be highly unlikely.

Yet, after all those years and all those suggestions, an absolutely convincing explanation for the men's disappearance is still teasingly elusive. For those who would still get to the bottom of the mystery it remains regrettable that, in the absence of recovered bodies and after months of studying reports by Superintendent Muirhead and others, the Crown decided in July 1901 not to hold an inquiry. 'After careful consideration,' went the announcement, 'Crown counsel have decided to take no further proceedings.'

The case may be officially closed, but the theories keep coming thick and fast. Hugh Munro, a teacher, writer and founder of the Flannan Isles Club – dedicated to keeping relatives of the keepers and other interested parties in touch with each other – long believed that 'there was some kind of cover-up'. Not a romantic by nature, having once helicoptered to the island and found it 'reasonably pleasant without provoking any uncomfortable eerie feeling as

Gibson's poem might have suggested'. But he instinctively felt there was something, somewhere that the public had not been informed about. And in particular, he pointed to an entry in the lighthouse visitors' book for 23 April, 1899.

On that day, eight months before the tragedy, Scott Moncrieff Penney had visited the light. His profession, given as 'advocate, Edinburgh', still looks conspicuously odd among the other entries by lightkeepers, seamen, works inspectors and the like. Why, wondered Munro, would he have taken the trouble to go all that way, across hazardous seas, for a social call? Wouldn't he have gone there for a professional reason?

Professor Robert Black, of Edinburgh University's department of Scots law, is more puzzled by Penney's job description and location, as at that point in his career according to Faculty of Advocates' records, Penney was a sheriff-substitute at Portree on the Isle of Skye. Black reckons that a good reason for his visiting the light would have been as a delegate for his sheriff-principal, who might have been too busy to fulfil his visiting obligation as a commissioner of northern lighthouses. The professor asserts that in those days sheriffs took a more active role than they do today in the prosecution of criminal cases, but he is wary of Munro's feeling that Penney might have been visiting the light on some kind of legal business that had alarmed one of the lightkeepers. 'Did that worry,' asked Munro, 'cause that keeper to eventually crack and confess something to his mates, a confession he later regretted and decided to nullify?'

But no-one now seems able to say with certainty what the sheriff-substitute was doing there – the lighthouse commissioners' office keeps no record of reasons for visits by anyone. However, the fact that Penney was accompanied on his trip by Peter Anderson, of Lighthouse Works (the only other name in the visitors' book on that date), suggests he might have been simply checking on contractors' execution of work on the light, which had then been in operation for only four months.

While accepting that possibility, Munro found another theory rather seductive – the idea that the lightkeepers might have seen something they should not have. Perhaps a potential enemy's new, top-secret warship? Even a revolutionary British craft on offshore trials? 'Perhaps its officers, realising that the wrong eyes had fallen upon them, sent out a party to cleanly and efficiently remove all risk of the sighting being reported... This would not necessarily have meant death of course. The men could simply have been kidnapped and later incarcerated, along with their forbidden knowledge, for the rest of their lives.'

Fantastic? Maybe, though it has to be said that stranger things have happened and that the men's disappearance in the first instance was strange enough in itself. Yet until the truth is somehow miraculously discovered, even the romantics will have to settle for the mundane. For when all is said and done and all outlandish theories discounted, set aside or exhausted, Superintendent Muirhead's matter-of-fact, death-by-drowning conclusion will doubtless become the accepted version of events, however unromantic its rather-too-logical assumption might be. And perhaps that is how it should be, for he was the man best qualified in professional and personal terms to have his opinion go down on the official record.

Indeed, he was not only a superior and colleague but also a friend of the dead men, and had hand-picked them for their important posts on the newly built lighthouse, designed by the author Robert Louis Stevenson's cousin. He wrote in his report:

I knew Ducat and Marshall intimately, and the Occasional McArthur well. I was with the keepers for a month during the summer of 1899 when everyone worked hard to secure the early lighting of the station before winter. The board has lost two of its most efficient keepers and a competent Occasional.

Principal keeper Ducat was 44 years old with 22 years' experience in the service, and the father of four children; assistant keeper Marshall was 30, with less than five years' experience; McArthur's age and experience were not on record, though, as a native of Lewis, he was a handy understudy – in this case for indisposed regular keeper William Ross, who was never able to return to Flannan after the tragedy.

He was not the only colleague deeply affected. Superintendent Muirhead himself was profoundly saddened by the affair, as the last man to see the lightkeepers alive just over a week before they vanished. His name and his wife's, appear in the visitors' book as the final guests to be entertained by the keepers. And with hindsight, it must have become a truly memorable occasion in their minds, for Muirhead concluded his report with genuinely touching words of sentiment:

I visited the Flannan Isles when the relief was made on December 7 and I have the melancholy recollection that I was the last person to shake hands with them and bid them adieu.

6

Trench's Fateful Case

WHERE THE SILVERY Tay opens out to the North Sea, where the well-to-do still live in their impressive high-windowed old houses on the north-eastern outskirts of Dundee, the suburban quiet was shattered at the dying end of 1912 by the revelation of the particularly brutal and apparently motiveless murder of a rich 65-year-old spinster, Miss Jean Milne. The oh so respectable neighbourhood was scandalised by the story. And it was to prove not only a story of one fatal tragedy, but also of a life ruined while it was still to be lived.

The killing of Miss Milne bore many similarities, disturbing but probably coincidental, to another notorious murder which had taken place in Glasgow a few years before; and not the least of these was the professional involvement of the most famous Scottish detective of his day, Detective-Lieutenant John Thomson Trench of the Glasgow City Police.

At the large Victorian mansion in Broughty Ferry where Miss Milne's body had been discovered, her head battered and her ankles bound with curtain cord, the Dundee police had found little or nothing to go on, and, swallowing their pride, felt they had no option but to yield to Trench's legendary talent and experience. The very fact that he was thus called in by the mystified local force was testament to the respect that Trench commanded among his colleagues in the Scottish police forces, though in some quarters nearer home it was to prove something of a grudging reaction, bordering dangerously on resentment.

The tenacious western lawman arrived in what must have been to him faraway, foreign east-coast territory two days after the investigation had begun. While he would doubtless have been flattered by the request for his services, it was a move that was to have a devastating effect on his 21-year career which, up to then, had been remarkably distinguished. So admired had he been for his efficiency and consistently brilliant performance that he had been awarded the King's Medal for meritorious service on the recommendation of his Chief Constable.

Even before he began to seek out what evidence there might be – without the benefit of Miss Milne's body, already removed for burial – Trench was drawing fateful parallels with that other case, the murder of Miss Marion Gilchrist in Glasgow in 1908, whose unsatisfactory resolution had become something of an obsession with him.

So many of the circumstances were the same: the respectable homes and the women's solitary lifestyles; the violent killings with blunt instruments (Milne with a poker, Gilchrist probably with a chair leg); the absence of theft, despite the accessibility of money and valuables; and the fact that neither home had been forcibly entered, implying that both victims had known their killers and admitted them willingly. But it was another similarity that emerged later that was to lead to Trench's downfall.

This was the willingness of various witnesses to come forward and swear, despite obviously less-than-perfect recall, that a mere suspect was 'definitely' the culprit. In the Gilchrist case, such witnesses had been responsible for the conviction of Oscar Slater, a Glasgow-based German gambler, and his sentencing to death for the Gilchrist murder – later commuted to life imprisonment – while other evidence that could have proved his innocence was conveniently ignored. Having been deeply involved in that case, Trench was convinced that a serious miscarriage of justice had taken place. Only for the sake of his job had he managed, with great difficulty, to keep his mouth shut.

When he saw history beginning to repeat itself in the Milne case, with the overriding desire to convict bringing on a similar blindness to the facts among his peers, Trench's conscience nagged him more intensely than ever and the temptation to loosen his tongue on the Gilchrist case began to lead him down the road to personal disaster.

Despite the recent appearance of modern residential developments on the early fringes of Broughty Ferry, there are still many imposing Victorian houses on, or just off, the leafy coast-hugging north road out of Dundee. Perched on the gentle riverbank that rolls down from the area's rich farming hinterland, a good number of these command a spectacular view across the Tay to the ancient Kingdom of Fife. This is the most discreetly well-off satellite of the city, where once the beneficiaries of its 19th century golden industrial age – the families of the jute factory bosses, for instance – retired quietly of an evening to enjoy and contemplate the fruits of their enterprise.

Elmgrove House was one such retreat. It now has a different name and a new role, as a residential home, and its 14 rooms are put to much more practical use than they once were – but, like so many other older residences that were built with no expense spared, the house has physically changed little since Jean Milne, sole sister and heiress of a wealthy Dundee tobacco manufacturer, lived out most of her solitary and abruptly foreshortened life within its echoing spaces. What changes there have been can only be called positive.

With its recessed gate punctuating head-high walls on a dog-leg corner of Grove Road between the high and low routes into Dundee, its boldly square architectural lines are softened by much overhanging greenery. While it is easy to imagine its looming presence behind the trees as shadowy and frightening in the days of gas street-lighting, today its once-grey stone walls have a bright surface of white paint that robs it of any lingering sinister aspect. And the gate is often wide open and, by implication, welcoming.

It was not so on Saturday, 2 November 1912, when the regular local postman found he could not get that morning's post into the overflowing letter-box. As Miss Milne usually notified him before going on holiday, his suspicions also overflowed – and he notified the police. One day later, after an inconclusive look at the premises the previous day – they were not over-keen to annoy the rather prickly old lady – they approached the house more determinedly. When there was no response to repeated ringing of the doorbell, a forced entry was made and, in the hall just beyond the front door, they were horrified to find the dead body of Miss Milne.

Lying at the foot of the stairs, it was fully dressed, partly covered with a sheet, and encircled by a pool of congealed blood that had obviously flowed freely from several head wounds. There was also a blood-stained poker beside it and the ankles had been tightly bound together with a cord from the nearby glass door's curtain – which had been arranged to obscure the scene from outside view. A few feet away the telephone wires had been cut, apparently with a pair of garden shears found close by.

While the state of the hall indicated there had been a violent struggle, the binding of the ankles seemed to suggest it had not been (immediately) to the death and that the old lady's assailant had left her alive, immobilising her to make a getaway. But what had been the motive? Nothing appeared to have gone missing from the house and her valuable rings were not removed from her fingers, so theft was ruled out. And yet...

Miss Milne was thought to be something of an eccentric locally and certainly had some strange habits – such as the use of candles for illumination, although the house was equipped with gas lighting – but the most notable thing about her was her wealth. Not only was she the owner of an extremely valuable house, inherited from her brother on his death nine years before, but she enjoyed what was then a remarkably high income of over £1,000 a year. It was not unreasonable to assume that her death was in some way connected to her wealth.

The local police were frankly baffled and, realising the similarity of the case to that of Marion Gilchrist, quickly called in the outstanding detective whose name had come to public prominence in relation to that investigation.

Detective-Lieutenant Trench arrived in Dundee within 24 hours of being summoned on the Monday, but was too late to stop the burial of Miss Milne's body the next day. He wasted no time in acquiring the pathologist's report of the post-mortem. This showed that death had occurred soon after the injuries were inflicted; that it had been caused by a combination of shock and cerebral haemorrhage brought on by numerous blows to the head, none of which was heavy enough in itself to be fatal; and that the advanced stage of decomposition indicated that at least three weeks had passed since the attack took place.

That seemed to square with the earliest postmark on Miss Milne's unretrieved mail – 14 October – but further enquiries began to complicate the date-of-death calculations. She was last seen alive on the 15th, and on the evening of the 16th a visiting church elder saw that the house was unusually dark and could get no response though he rang and knocked. Three nights later a trunk call from London also failed to get a reply, so it was deduced that Miss Milne must have met her demise on the night of October 15/16. However, her late brother's former gardener, Alexander Troup, later claimed that when he called at the house on 21 October to collect a contribution for charity, he saw a woman – whom he assumed to be Miss Milne – moving a curtain at an upper window. But he also failed to get a response. Neither did he succeed when he returned in the afternoon to try again. This time he noticed that the cover of the front-door lock, which in the forenoon had been down, was now up, inferring that in the meantime a key had been inserted.

This honest man's statement and other incidental details, such as the covering of the body with a sheet and the series of relatively light blows to the head, prompted a school of thought that the date of death had been later and that the culprit was a woman. Intriguing though that theory appeared, Trench's instinct compelled him to stick with the conclusion of the autopsy, although there was something odd about that too.

Failing to have the body exhumed, he nevertheless managed to examine the woman's clothes. He noticed several strange double punctures in them that appeared to have come from jabs by a two-pronged carving-fork – such as had been found beneath a trunk in the hall but dismissed as irrelevant. There was no doubt that it would have made corresponding marks on the body. So why had this connection not been made? Indeed, the acknowledgement of more 'light' wounds would have supported a 'female culprit' theory. Yet it remained one to which Trench could not subscribe, and gradually the evidence began to accumulate on the 'male' side.

Trench soon unearthed a significant prop to his case, which had been previously overlooked. Raking around the ashes of the dining-room grate, he recovered a partly smoked cigar. Putting this together with the fact that just before her death the lonely Miss Milne had set the dining-room table for two, and later evidence that she had ordered a supply of wine from a local dealer 'of the same quality as my brother used to get', he felt there could be no doubt about the killer's gender.

A reward of £100 was offered for information that would lead to an arrest and witnesses came forward thick and fast to confirm that Miss Milne had been enjoying the attentions of at least one handsome male stranger. Two of her female friends said she had confided in them about a new man in her life and she had been so 'girlish' about it that they had concluded the relationship was a romantic one.

The maid of a neighbouring house said she had seen, from her upstairs window, a handsome six-foot-tall man in evening dress 'walking up and down' Elmgrove's garden paths one morning in the second week of October.

Elmgrove's occasional gardener recalled receiving a stranger at the house – just before Miss Milne was due to tour the Highlands in September – whom she welcomed with an excited cry: 'You have come!' He was 40ish, about five feet nine inches tall, with a cheery face, fair hair and slight moustache. He wore a tweed hat, was of 'gentlemanly aspect' and had a deep, guttural voice, which led the gardener to assume that he was the 'charming German' Miss Milne had mentioned meeting on one of her occasional trips to London.

Other witnesses who saw 'a strange man' around the

entrance of the house included two local sisters (7 October) and a group of playing boys (11 October). But perhaps the following two were the most significant, taking account of the dates.

A Dundee taxi-driver recalled picking up an 'English' fare from the West Station in the early hours of 15 October who wanted to go to Broughty Ferry and asked to be dropped off in the vicinity of Elmgrove. He was so agitated and 'sinister' that the cabbie was relieved to part company with this tallish man who carried a small bag, wore an overcoat and a waterproof and had a slight fair moustache.

And a dustman claimed that, while at work in Grove Road at about 4.30 on the morning of 16 October, he had seen a bowler-hatted man come out of the house gate. This individual had drawn back on realising he had been seen, then emerged again to walk briskly away and round the corner. He was tall, about 30, with a thin pale face and a slight fair moustache.

Among the many confusing elements of these similar but incomplete descriptions was the question of accents. These were variously cited as German, English and American. From the unopened post in Miss Milne's letter-box (mostly begging letters) the local police had retrieved something that prompted them to contact Scotland Yard about the whereabouts of 'a dashing American'. This was almost certainly a factor in the near-downfall of a certain Charles Warner, of 210 Wilton Avenue, Toronto.

When the hue and cry reached the police at Maidstone in Kent, Mr Warner happened to be in their custody. He also happened, more or less, to fit the descriptions supplied. It did not seem to matter that he had been detained for nothing more serious than the non-payment of a seven shilling restaurant bill. Maidstone police were convinced that they had Miss Milne's murderer on their hands and promptly had him photographed. What was later to be described as 'an exceptionally bad' mugshot was then forwarded to Scotland for identification by the local witnesses.

On the strength of a general consensus of recognition among them, the chosen five – the gardener, the maid, the sisters, and the dustman – were dispatched to Maidstone to effect identification in the flesh. But where was the taxi driver, with his most vital evidence? It seems he simply wasn't invited, and that was as good a reason as any for Lieutenant Trench's doubts.

The hospitality extended to them included a sightseeing tour of London, and the witnesses were most co-operative at the identification parade – described by an angry Warner as 'a farce'. With the exception only of the maid, who expressed doubts about his 'too grey' hair, they all pronounced the prisoner to be The Man. A warrant for his arrest was obtained from the Dundee Sheriff, and Lieutenant Trench, with the document and a pair of handcuffs in his pocket, travelled south.

As Warner left prison after serving his 14 days for the restaurant offence, he was surprised to be met by a welcoming committee which included curious members of the public, press photographers, the local chief constable – who immediately charged him with Miss Milne's murder – and Trench, whose snapping-on of the handcuffs was accompanied by a battery of cameras clicking. 'You'll be sorry for this in a few days,' protested Warner. 'I'm an innocent man.'

Before he and Trench left for Dundee, Warner had to suffer one more indignity. At Scotland Yard he was confronted with six local witnesses who claimed to have seen Miss Milne in the company of the 'dashing American' at the Strand Palace and Bonnington hotels. But not one of them was prepared to say Warner was the man. It was a different story, however, on his arrival in Scotland.

After he appeared before the Sheriff to be formally charged – and closely examined by the local press, which described him as 'muscular, well-groomed and of gentlemanly appearance, with the only drawback to his attractiveness being his unshaved condition' – a fresh batch of no fewer than 22 'witnesses' was produced for yet another identification exercise. Among them were the playing boys, two ladies who saw 'the man' with Miss Milne on a west coast cruise, a local hairdresser who removed the moustache of a well-dressed man about the middle of October... but no taxi driver. The results were not officially made public, but it was repeatedly stated in the press that a dozen witnesses had made positive identifications.

It is not difficult to imagine what the fair-minded Lieutenant Trench must by now have been thinking, in view not only of his growing general unhappiness about the reliability of recognition sworn by so-called witnesses, but especially considering the revealing conversations he had had with Warner on their long train journey from London to Dundee's Tay Bridge station. There had been plenty of time to hear the case for the defence in the greatest of detail.

Even before he began to study the incognito 'Mr Brown' with whom he was travelling literally in tandem, Trench found himself resisting that post-arrest triumphant feeling many officers might have yielded to; he was simply not satisfied that this was 'a fair cop'.

Warner protested that he had never been to Scotland in his life and that his avoidance of the restaurant bill in Tonbridge had been prompted by hungry desperation after he had miscalculated his budget on a tour of France, Holland, Belgium and England. So where, asked Trench, had he been on the crucial date of 16 October? 'Antwerp,' said Warner.

'How long had you been there?' asked Trench, who by now was warming to the young Canadian, who was handling his misfortune with an easy, almost jaunty air. Trench no doubt hoped this optimism was not based on a misplaced faith in himself or, worse, in British justice.

Warner replied that he had lived in the Flemish city for a week before the murder date and had left on the 17th, arriving in London on the 18th. 'Can you prove it?' asked Trench. Warner shook his head and explained that he had been sleeping rough. Then he suddenly remembered that, on the relevant date, he had pawned a waistcoat in Antwerp for one franc. Did he still have the ticket? Yes! He handed it over to Trench, knowing in a way, that he was also handing over his fate to him.

Aware that with statements from no fewer than 100 witnesses, Dundee's Procurator Fiscal was already submitting his prepared case to the Crown in Edinburgh for the framing of the indictment on which Warner would be brought to trial, Trench knew what he had to do – and do quickly. Soon, he was on a train again, returning south; then travelling east by ship to Belgium's Flemish capital-of-the-north. And there, his detective's natural enterprise undeterred by the confusing network of 16th century buildings, he quickly found Warner's pawnshop.

He redeemed the waistcoat, allowed himself a little self-congratulation, and headed home with Warner's perfect alibi tucked under his arm in a brown paper parcel. The effect, on his return, was dramatic and immediate. With the prosecution's guns so effectively spiked, the Crown Office could hardly allow the case to go ahead. It thus sent the following telegram to the Fiscal:

> CHARLES WARNER ... MURDER ... CROWN COUNSEL HAVE CONSIDERED PRECOGNITIONS AND DECIDED EVIDENCE INSUFFICIENT ... PLEASE LIBERATE.

Warner's words of gratitude to Trench for the return of his waistcoat and his liberty are not on record, but this happy development was to mean a lot more to Trench than a smiling thank-you and a handshake. Though he was never to bring the true culprit to justice, the experience had proved to him that a false trail could be corrected. And perhaps that could still be achieved, however belatedly, for the wrongly convicted Oscar Slater? In that case too, there had been nothing whatsoever to connect the accused to the crime but the doubtful 'identification' of witnesses. And the Milne affair had confirmed for Trench that such evidence, while clearly worthless, could nevertheless condemn an innocent man to the gallows. Now his conscience simply would not rest.

The postscript to this story is a sad one. To appreciate the irony of it, some details of the Gilchrist murder should be noted. The old lady was killed when her maid, Nellie Lambie, left the house to buy a newspaper – and returned to find a curious neighbour at the door, Arthur Adams, who had been alerted by 'chopping noises' from within. They entered the house to be confronted by a man who swept past 'like greased lightning'; and when they found the dead body of her mistress, Adams raced down into the street to give chase but could not see the man. Adams later said that Lambie did not seem surprised by the man's presence and he therefore thought that she must have known him.

This was Trench's belief too. Involved in the case from the start, he knew that Lambie had named as the intruder not Slater but another man known to her. However, something else she said had sent Trench's superiors off on a different trail from which they were not to be deflected by mere logic. The only valuable item missing from the house, she claimed, was a diamond crescent brooch. And it was discovered that Slater had been trying to sell a pawn ticket for such a brooch around the gaming houses he frequented.

This was surely their man! Not only did he live near the murder scene, but he had been known to use several different names and had also suddenly left Glasgow for New York. The inconvenient facts that the brooch 1) when recovered from the pawnshop, did not resemble the stolen one, and 2) had been pawned long before the murder, were simply brushed aside. Slater was brought back from America and charged with Marion Gilchrist's murder. Now Nellie Lambie, and several other witnesses, were prepared to say he was the man, though Arthur Adams was more cautious.

No-one was interested in Trench's protests, or Slater's for that matter – 'My lord, I know nothing about the affair, you are convicting an innocent man' – and the prisoner was sentenced to be hanged on 27 May 1909. Though massive public protests were perhaps responsible for this being commuted to life imprisonment two days before it was carried out, the bewildered man was taken to Peterhead Prison where, as Convict No. 1992, he was to spend nearly two decades begging for justice.

Although several distinguished pens fought bravely to expose the flaws in the prosecution's case against him – including those of the famous criminologist William Roughead and the creator of Sherlock Holmes, Sir Arthur Conan Doyle – nothing was done in high places for Oscar Slater as the early years of his imprisonment passed. He was not to know that his best champion was to be a Glasgow policeman who, after the Broughty Ferry affair, was about to put his distinguished career on the line for him.

Initially, Trench himself did not even know that. He knew, of course, that to challenge his police superiors directly would be perceived as an unforgivable professional sin – as would an approach over their heads to a higher authority. But it was a straight choice. And reckoning that the first course would find stony ground in any case, what he had to do was pursue the latter with 'safety' guarantees attached. Eventually, a prominent lawyer, David Cook, persuaded a prison commissioner to put Trench's plea discreetly to Scottish Secretary McKinnon Wood. The response – 'If the constable mentioned will send me a written statement of the evidence in his possession, I will give this matter my best consideration' – led the detective to believe that he could impart his information with impunity.

He was utterly and naively wrong.

Though Cook pressured the Scottish Secretary into setting up an enquiry into the Slater case, this was commonly seen as a farce. When its results were later published as a parliamentary paper, it was riddled with asterisks where evidence had been deemed inconvenient and the key name of the man first given by Lambie – a name still much argued about in Glasgow – appeared only as initials.

Trench recalled a niece of Miss Gilchrist, quoting Lambie just after the murder: 'Oh, Miss Birrell, I think it was AB. I know it was AB.' And he mentioned a visit to Lambie when he 'touched on AB', asking if she really thought this was the man she saw. Her answer was: 'It's gey funny if it wasn't him

I saw.' Yet both these witnesses now denied ever having made such statements and, to compound Trench's predicament, one Glasgow policeman after another came forward to discredit his evidence.

As the farce ended on 25 April, Trench's troubles really began. With no action being taken on Slater's conviction, the detective was suspended from duty three months later, the case going before the Glasgow magistrates along with this statement from his Chief Constable: 'It is contrary to public policy and to all police practice for an officer to communicate to persons outside the police force information which he has acquired in the course of his duty, without the express sanction of the chief officer of his force.'

Trench defended himself and his altruistic motives robustly, but even production of the Scottish Secretary's letter asking for his information failed to save him. He was dismissed with ignominy from the Glasgow police on 14 September 1914. An appeal to McKinnon Wood had no effect – the Scottish Secretary did not even bother to respond to his letter.

Surely his enemies in the force were satisfied? Not so, it appears. Although he enlisted in the Royal Scots Fusiliers to start building a new career for himself, his ex-colleagues were not finished with John Thomson Trench. As a parting shot, they mounted what was later described as a 'vindictive' prosecution against him and the lawyer Cook, accusing them of receiving stolen goods while Trench was with the force. But this time they were thwarted. The judge dismissed the case, saying that the men, who had been concerned with returning the goods to their rightful owners, had actually acted with 'meritorious intention'.

The once-great detective never recovered from the double shock. Though he served his regiment well throughout the

Great War with the rank of quartermaster-sergeant, he died at the age of 50, on the fourth anniversary of his arrest. He did not, therefore, live to see Oscar Slater released some ten years later.

On 10 November 1927, the then Scottish Secretary Sir John Gilmour finally gave in to pressure from the media to authorise Slater's release, already overdue in terms of the average span of 'life'. But if Sir John was expecting applause for the decision, he did not get it. Even as a relieved, if disbelieving, Slater was telling the press 'I want rest, I want rest' – outside the Glasgow rabbi's home to which he had been invited to pick up his life again – the media pressure was renewed, this time for an appeal hearing to clear Slater's name. Again, the authorities yielded, and at last the original court judgement was 'set aside'.

Disappointingly for Slater, who hoped to be unequivocally cleared, this was based on a technicality; yet he received £6,000 compensation. He owed a lot to Sir Arthur Conan Doyle, who had campaigned for him to the end, but they fell out, and his gratitude, in the form of a £200 gift, was focused on an equally deserving sympathiser, journalist William Park. An old friend of Trench, he was the man largely responsible for the effectiveness of the last barrage of pressure with the publication of his book, *The Truth About Oscar Slater*.

He was also the only man who fully realised the contribution of his friend, acknowledged in the book's dedication with words that ring as a fitting epitaph to a man who gave his life to justice but received little of it in return:

Dedicated to the memory of the late Lieutenant John T Trench, King's Medallist, Glasgow, who, as a public officer of the police force, actuated by an inspiring sense of justice, sacrificed his career and pension in a personal attempt to rescue from a life's detention in prison, and with a desire to save others from the risk of a similar cruel fate, a man whom he believed on his conscience to have been wrongly convicted in the Scottish High Court of Justiciary, and for which noble act he was dismissed and ruined.

7

Gone Like a Ghost

CROFTER CALUM CAMERON turned his weather-beaten face away, looked to the heavens in exasperation, and closed his eyes to the bright sunshine. He was obviously a man who enjoyed and craved peace. And his now-expired life lived out in a simple two-storey cottage with four dormer windows looking over a sandy inlet to the open sea – would have been delightfully quiet, even by the standards of the holy island of Iona, were it not for that fateful night in November 1929, when his parents' boarder, Norah Emily Farnario, walked out into the darkness clutching a knife in her hand.

He was only 12 years old at the time, growing up in what many would consider an idyllic setting: a playground of gardens and fields, rocks and beaches, animals and fishing; in a world of his own set apart (by perhaps half a mile) from what is still today a close-knit community of cottages along the shore-front where the little ferry comes in across the one-and-a-half-mile Sound of Iona from Fionnphort on Mull. No doubt he also ventured further, along the encircling island track, to the large green mound of Fairy Hill, said to harbour the spirits of the pre-Christian dead; the mystic mound that seemed to fascinate Miss Farnario so.

At first sight, viewed from the ferry, the island of Iona seems nothing much more than pleasingly pretty. In contrast to the elemental and mountainous magnificence of its near-neighbour Mull, it is small, green and low and, were it not for its silver sands, handsomely restored abbey and historic founding role in the establishment of Christianity in Scotland – St Columba and 12 companions landed there in 563 AD – it would be but a pleasant, unimportant dot on the map of Scotland.

With its many landmarks bearing deep and sometimes puzzling significance in the history of religion, the island has become a place of pilgrimage not only for believers and students of theology from all over the world, but also for tourists whose presence is philosophically accepted by the resident islanders – fewer than a hundred – who are by nature reticent and matter-of-fact and practise their own faith in that modest spirit.

While the presence of the young Iona Community might compound this slightly uneasy mix, its spiritual idealism is remarkably effective in breathing new life into the island. The abbey, lovingly restored, is a haven for people once more; and the little school that almost died a few decades ago is again and echoing to the cries of human regeneration behind the ruins of the ancient nearby nunnery. But Iona was not so lively and cosmopolitan when Miss Farnario, accompanied by a lady friend who would soon leave her to her own fateful devices, made her pilgrimage from London in August 1928; then it was still an island in the fullest sense of the word, far from anywhere, without basic amenities and communication systems.

Paradoxically, that probably uplifted the tall, rather intense young woman in hand-woven clothes as, after more than two days of travelling, she and her companion stepped off the ferry into a different world, yet one which she imagined she knew well, for her basic motivation for making the daunting journey to Iona was the belief that she had been on the island in a previous incarnation. She intended to stay for an indefinite period to seek the peace and serenity that had eluded her in London and, as she made her way along the shorefront to the house of Mrs Macdonald where she would be boarding, no doubt she felt some of that already washing over her. She would use the quiet to write about, and pursue her study of, telepathy, faith-healing and other mystical subjects. She would use it also to find some quietness in herself. But that was not to be.

Norah Farnario, the 32-year-old troubled daughter of an Italian doctor and an English gentlewoman, may have physically escaped from the city, but she was not to struggle free from the dark forces that inhabited her own mind. These came with her like so much unwanted baggage; and if she had hoped to find a place whose force for peace would do battle with and overcome the demons, she had come to the wrong place.

Superficially perhaps, Iona exudes serenity but it is a strangely powerful peace. As Kenneth Clark wrote in *Civilisation,* when trying to capture the potency of the island's atmosphere, 'I never come to Iona without the feeling that some god is in this place'. And Mrs Alison Johnson, of the St Columba Hotel on the track up to the abbey, puts it this way: 'Iona is a strong place. It can attract some 'interesting' types and, if people are a little unbalanced when they arrive here, it can overbalance them completely.'

Certainly, something like that happened to the darkly attractive Miss Farnario – for, far from finding inner quiet in the simple life in Iona, she seemed to suffer increasing mental anguish the longer she stayed. She was always restless. After her companion departed, she moved from her lodgings in the east to Traighmor, the Camerons' relatively isolated croft, about half-a-mile to the south-west of the main cluster of village houses. But despite its delightful location, set back from a small, craggy bay behind a hundred-metre expanse of lush grass, she could find no peace there either.

By day, she was often to be seen sitting down by the shore writing; and although her thoughts were obviously deep and obsessional, she never attempted to impose them upon islanders or visitors, to whom she was friendly, charming and consequently well liked. When she felt she could, she would mix freely among them, and she appreciated the fact that they respected her privacy. Yet, however comfortable and popular she became with them, she remained less than comfortable with herself. For by night, it was a different and less congenial story. She went out, with increasing frequency, on lonely walks to study the island's ancient, mysterious mounds and stones, fuelling her preoccupation with spiritualism and the occult.

Given the atmospheric power of the place even by day, perhaps it was not surprising that the forces of darkness came down heavily upon her. She seemed, almost, to be asking for trouble and was particularly fascinated by the mound known in the Gaelic as Sìthean Mòr, the Fairy Hill, a grassy knoll just south of the extremity of the road leading to the machair, a tract of arable land in the middle west of the island. As its ancient name suggests, the mound is one of several knolls of pre-Christian times in Iona where, according to legend, the fairies or angels would revel while passing mortals heard the faint strains of their music emanating from within. Here also, a prying monk is said to have witnessed St Columba himself in communion with the angels – 'Clad in white garments, they came flying to him with wonderful speed,' relates his biographer Adomnan, 'and stood round the holy man as he prayed.' Here also, Norah Farnario joined the angels.

Talking after that sad event, Miss Varney, her housekeeper in the family home at Mortlake Road, Kew, described her mistress as 'a woman of extraordinary character who claimed to cure people by telepathy' and who, despite being quite cheerful and happy much of the time, would 'moan and cry out piteously' if not allowed to heal someone she perceived as having a curable problem. She had once announced her intention of fasting for 40 days but was persuaded to give up after two weeks. Occasionally, she 'went off into trances for several hours'.

Miss Farnario is said to have told her hosts at Traighmor that they should not be alarmed if she should go into a trance for as long as a week. Not surprisingly, Calum's family began to wonder about their endearing but ever-more-disturbed young guest from London.

Apart from her strange nocturnal walks, there were other disturbing behaviours: her increasingly agitated demeanour that manifested itself in growing dishevelment; incoherent references to visions and spiritual messages; the fact that her curtains were never drawn because she believed she could see the faces of her previous 'patients' in the clouds; and the two oil lamps that she kept burning in her room throughout the night. She did not, apparently, get much sleep. If she were not out walking, she would write by the light of these lamps far into the night and was often so exhausted by dawn that she would then go to bed for the rest of the day. When she seemed particularly overwrought, the Camerons would consider calling a doctor – but were specifically warned against that by their guest. Presumably because of her convictions, or perhaps because of some difference with her doctor-father, she had no time for practitioners of orthodox medicine

It was thus difficult to know what precisely was ailing

her and in the absence of qualified medical enlightenment, the villagers could do no more than hazard guesses at her condition. Despite their sympathy for her, some of these were less than respectful. At the very least, she was considered to have a severe persecution complex. But did she even know herself what the problem was? To her, no doubt, the demons inside her head were more than imaginings. She behaved as if she was being hunted, and if her pursuers were not evil spirits of her own creation, who, or what, were they?

In any case, the hunting was to come to an abrupt and shocking conclusion as the winter of 1929 drew in.

It must have been something of a relief to the Camerons when, on Sunday, 17 November, their guest rose unusually early and dramatically announced that she would have to leave the island, having received messages to that effect 'from the world beyond'. When the Camerons realised that she intended to go immediately, they warned her that this would be impossible: there were no ferries running on the Sabbath. This did not seem to get through to her until, packed up and standing by the shore, she saw for herself – gazing across the Sound to Mull – that there was no way she could get off the island that day.

Frightened and dejected, she returned to the cottage, announced that she had had another call and was not now leaving, then locked herself in her room. When she reappeared briefly before going to bed, however, the hunted look was gone and she seemed unusually rational and normal. 'Aye,' recalled Calum, 'she was all right on the Sunday night.'

But she was certainly not all right the next morning. When Calum's sister took breakfast to her room, she did not answer the knock. There was a smell of burning, so the girl entered, to find the room empty. The bedclothes were turned down from the pillows, the oil lamps near her typewriter were still alight, and the fireplace was filled with burned papers and pamphlets. All her clothing was still in the room and such personal belongings as her watch, rings, and hairpins lay neatly on the dressing-table. Nothing appeared to be missing.

The Camerons, alarmed, searched the neighbourhood and called out for her along the shore where she had been in the habit of sitting. But there was no trace of their lonely lodger. Remembering that she had gone missing before, they then waited for a few hours – perhaps she'd just over-extended one of her nocturnal walks – before summoning a group of neighbourly helpers, whose efforts also proved fruitless.

She was still missing when darkness fell, and next morning the search, now scaled up with official police support from Mull and more island volunteers, got under way again. But it was not until the Tuesday afternoon that the breakthrough came. Alerted by their excited collie, two farmers announced that they had seen 'something white' on the side of Fairy Hill. And when the searchers drew close, they gasped with shock at the sight of Norah Farnario's naked body. A *Glasgow Bulletin* informant described the scene like this:

> The body was lying in a sleeping posture on the right side, the head resting on the right hand. Round the neck was a silver chain and cross. A few feet away a knife was found. Miss Farnario had left the Camerons' farmhouse (about a mile away) sometime during Sunday night. The island was bathed in moonlight and a very keen frost prevailed. The doctor who was called gave it as his opinion that death was due to exposure. With the exception of a few scratches on the feet, caused by walking over the rough ground, there were no marks on the body.

And a reporter for the *Oban Times* gave this version:

> Her body, which was unclothed, was discovered lying on
> a large cross which had been cut out of the turf, apparent-
> ly with a knife which was lying by, and round her neck
> was a silver chain and cross. Death was apparently due
> to exposure.

Other accounts further elaborated the basic facts. She was
not completely naked – she wore a black cloak decorated
with occult insignia. The silver chain around her neck was
no longer silver – it had turned black. She had taken the long
steel knife in the age-old belief that the simple act of carrying
a blade would ward off evil spirits; it was not lying beside
her but had to be forcibly removed from her tightly clutched
fingers. Alternatively, some suggest the knife was for fending
off a real rather than an imagined danger. 'The balls of her feet
were badly bruised' as if she had been desperately running
away from something or someone. It was rumoured that a
'man in a cloak' had been seen in the vicinity.

There were many highly developed theories, but Calum
Cameron, in his down-to-earth way, always shrugged off
fanciful speculation. 'It was just an ordinary kitchen knife,'
he said, 'which could have done no harm to anybody.' He
was clearly not impressed by the knife-for-defence theory and
believed her fate was sealed only by the frost. 'She just died of
exposure as the doctor said, it's that simple.' So the knife was
only for cutting that symbolic cross in the turf? 'There was
no cross,' he claimed. 'She was just digging in the ground,
maybe trying to get to the fairies inside. She was a disturbed
woman, that's all.'

Indeed, foul play was ruled out and the cause of death was

officially stated to be heart failure. But others have found the story of Miss Farnario's bizarre death less easy to explain, one of these being her London housekeeper, who was clearly perplexed by the prescient note she received from her mistress two days before her death. It said simply:

My dear Miss Varney – Do not be surprised if you do not hear from me for a very long time. I have a terrible healing case on.

One school of thought believed Miss Farnario had been a victim of 'psychic murder'. Having dabbled in spiritualism, theosophy, mind-reading and faith healing to the point of joining the Alpha and Omega occult group, she had also become friendly with the wife of Samuel Liddell Mathers, a leading light of another group of occultists, The Golden Dawn. The alleged penalty for breaking this group's oath of silence was to be subjected to 'a current of will' which would cause the offender 'to fall dead or paralysed as if blasted by lightning'.

So had the victim been so indiscreet as to make herself the target of what a leading figure in the occult world called an 'astral attack'? Was her increasingly agitated behaviour caused by some perceived threat of such a fate? Was she pursued by the cloaked man to her death? Did she commit a kind of passive suicide? The answers are now buried with Norah Emily Farnario in the graveyard of kings at St Odhrain's chapel in the grounds of Iona Abbey, where a tiny, mossy open-book memorial yields only the line:

N.E.F. Aged 33. 19th Nov 1929

She was interred three days after being found. Through papers discovered in her room, an uncle and aunt were contacted in London but no member of her family was able to journey to Scotland, and a solicitor was sent to make the necessary arrangements. In contrast, the tragedy and pathos of her premature death had so aroused the sympathies of the islanders that, according to one visitor's account, 'practically every soul on Iona attended her impressive funeral'.

While the mysteries of her harrowing life and death may have gone with her, what is certain is that the troubled young woman who went to seek peace in Iona did finally find it there. The ultimate peace.

8

The Ship of Death

HE WAS A short-trousered lad then, head down in his classroom at St Mary's School, earnestly getting down to serious work after a playful lunch-break. But when the huge explosion occurred, like a great thunder cracking across the River Clyde less than a mile-and-a-half away, he was immediately on his feet again, shocked and confused and ready to run. He couldn't understand what was happening as the windows of the schoolroom blew a shattering of glass inwards across the desks and his classmates screamed.

'We didn't realise the implications of it at the time,' recalled Tony McGlone more than half a century later. And neither did his name-forgotten teacher, though her unflappability made its mark on his memory:

> She ordered us all to stay put, stay calm, and we tried to keep on working, but it was difficult; and as soon as school was out, we all ran down to the esplanade to see what had caused the huge bang.

What Tony McGlone and his schoolmates beheld that Tuesday afternoon, gazing in transfixed shock across the water from the riverbank road that skirts the gritty old shipbuilding town of Greenock – of which he was to become the provost in later life – was a pall of smoke rising from a large warship in the naval anchorage off Princes Pier. They were by no means the only onlookers: many local shops had taken a half-day holiday and it seemed as if the whole population of the town had gathered to watch. They saw the estuary alive with chaotic drama-charged activity. Other big ships, having weighed anchor and moved away to safer waters, had sent small launches to assist in the rescue operations. But already the situation looked bad. The stricken ship was, as recalled by Tony, 'well on fire and listing badly' as rescue teams tried desperately to snatch her crewmen to safety before she broke up and sank. It was to be a losing battle, with a tragic toll of many young lives, and 'long after the war you could still see her remaining mast and the top of one of her funnels protruding from the water'.

The date was 30 April 1940, and what he had witnessed was the frantic aftermath of the mysterious (self?)-destruction of the *Maillé-Brézé,* a 2,440-ton French Cassard class destroyer, which had come to 'rest' in the Clyde after acquitting herself with honour at the Battle of Narvik. In this critical episode of the war, both British and French had been attempting to prevent the fall of Norway by landing British troops on its coast. The *Maillé-Brézé* had fought alongside British vessels, helping to knock out all eight German destroyers engaged against them, to effect what turned out to be a too-brief Allied landing. She was one of four French destroyers to be mentioned in dispatches for the brave and skilful performance of her 220-strong crew.

It was thus supremely ironic that, having survived such a bruising and decisive battle, she was to meet a surprisingly violent end in the friendly and relatively peaceful waters of the Clyde, a few miles west of Glasgow. She had arrived three days before, along with a couple of Royal Navy warships, to enjoy the naval equivalent of a boxer's pause between rounds: the most welcome part of conflict, the clean-up and refreshment, which in maritime terms meant refuelling, replenishing, re-ammunitioning, and general maintenance.

There should have been nothing dangerous in that. So how did the ship suddenly explode and, consequently, lose many of her young crewmen in an agonising death?

Among her impressive array of armaments, the eight-year-old *Maillé-Brézé* boasted six 21.7-inch torpedo tubes, and it was generally reported by survivors that during maintenance work on one of these, 'something happened', a torpedo came adrift, flew out of the tube, skidded along the deck, and collided with the lower structure of the bridge, causing the enormous explosion that reverberated through Greenock and as far as ten miles beyond.

For the many brave local people who dashed to the scene without hesitation – all kinds of small vessels cast off from Princes Pier and Albert Harbour to join forces with the professionals' boats from the nearby warships – there was no time to ask: why? Dunkirk was yet two months away, but its spirit was already to be seen here as waves of wounded crewmen, many of them badly burned, were ferried to safety. Some were taken to other ships at anchor, others were treated immediately on the small boats even as they were being taken ashore. And by the time the first casualties reached land, ambulances were waiting to take them to hospital.

Even when there was a gap in the ambulance relays, succour was at hand. A general alert having been sent out to Air Raid Protection posts, dozens of volunteers, including many nurses, were standing by at the docks to administer first aid to the injured. The close-knit community of Greenock was pulling out all the stops. For the shocked but not too badly hurt, a comfort station was set up in the Greenock Temperance Institute, where local women, with perspiration pouring down their faces, ministered to the young Frenchmen as if they were their own sons. Hot drinks and plates of food were handed out, and an interpreter was produced – Mrs McGill, a Frenchwoman who had married a Greenock man. But, as a local newspaper put it when recording the event five years later after the lifting of wartime censorship: 'Frenchman and Scot did not need to speak a common language that day. Each knew what the other wanted, and many a Frenchman, by a silent handshake, spoke more deeply of his gratitude than in words.'

In response to the dreadful event, the best side of human nature had emerged in a tragic kind of triumph. Brotherly love, compassion and courage rose up everywhere. For some, however, there was to be no salvation; no joyful landing on shore; no chance to express gratitude for local people's courage. For as the catalogue of dramas unfolded, it became clear that a number of unfortunate sailors on the *Maillé-Brézé* had somehow got hopelessly trapped below – in the forward mess-deck near the potentially lethal unflooded main magazine – and their chances of being saved were minimal. Indeed, their grim plight so perplexed their would-be rescuers that old men are, to this day, moved to tears by the memory. It had been truly unbearable to witness, for it transpired that there was simply no way to save the men, no way they could be brought out of the holocaust... because the forecastle hatch from the deck had been buckled by the first explosion and fire raged between them and the bulkhead door leading aft. The final horror of the situation was that, while a few of them could stick their heads out of the portholes to gasp for air, the holes were too small for the slimmest of men to crawl through.

As it was, frustrated by their own powerlessness in the face of the French sailors' harrowing screams for help, the rescuers soon began clutching at straws. A desperate plan emerged to cut through the ship's hull with oxyacetylene gear, but as a group of suitably-equipped men approached on the duty cutter from HMS *Warspite,* they were waved away by a British officer who had boarded the blazing ship. Lieutenant DS Johnston, from HMS *Furious,* reckoned there was too little time to effect such a precarious and complicated operation successfully, and the danger of a blow-back that would cost more lives was too great. Things had looked even worse from the vantage point he had bravely climbed to, the better to assess the situation.

And he wasn't alone. With shells from the ready-use lockers looping and bursting all around them, he and four other Royal Navy men – including Lieutenant RH Roberts, a probationary temporary-surgeon – had risked their own lives to shin up the ship's massive anchor chain from their own small boat and lever themselves over the high, red-hot bow. They reckoned that from there, with a brisk northerly breeze sweeping the fire aft along the hull that was lying north-and-south in the estuary, they would at least be able to see how and who they could help.

But it did not look good from the moment they stepped on deck. One of the boarding sailors, Able Seaman Robert McCaw, made straight for the jammed forecastle hatch cover and optimistically applied his brute strength to it; but it simply refused to budge and, as his fingers began to burn unbearably, he had to admit defeat. He stood up with a deep sigh and addressed his eyes to Johnston: what now? Confronted with danger and distress from all angles – the suffocating French sailors beseeching them for help from the portholes, the unexploded main magazine threatening them from below, a torpedo warhead burning but not exploding a few feet away – the lieutenant realised that very little could be done. And the decision was up to him. He looked at Roberts the surgeon, already preparing his hypodermic needle and morphine phials, and with an air of grim resignation reluctantly gave him the nod.

The doctor took off his uniform jacket, stretched his body out and over the searing edge of the deck, and called out to the men below: would they please extend their arms – not their heads – from the portholes? When his intention was understood, there was a general scuffling and crying, 'like trapped rats tearing at each other to get away first', it was said later. But who could blame them? A more dreadful fate by far was fast overtaking them. Roberts grabbed the first arm, squeezed home the sedative, and pulled himself back quickly to roll over and reload the syringe. Then he took another, pulled back and reloaded; then another until, after a few dying cries, all at once the ship fell ominously silent. Together, the hypnotic sedative and the overpowering heat and fumes from the holocaust had finally done their work. 'At about 1600 hours,' it was later reported to the Admiralty, 'there were no living men inboard.'

It might not have brought about a joyful resolution, but surgeon Roberts' remarkable act of mercy was to be long remembered as one of the most heroic episodes of that fateful day; at the very least it had brought blessed, ultimate relief to many desperate men facing a horrific end. Little wonder that, equally, it had been a relief to him and his fellow-rescue workers to hear no more the agonised moans and screams of the hapless victims as they succumbed to the roasting heat and deadly fumes. Doubtless, they would have preferred a quick end; but such was the contrary mood of the gods that disastrous day, the one miracle that took place only made things worse for the trapped men: they must have wondered why, amid all the fires of hell, the nearby unflooded main magazine – only recently restocked with a potent mix of shells, torpedo warheads and depth-charges – had not blown up and blasted them away with one merciful blow.

But there was a deal more courage to be seen that day; not least among the men of the regular fire brigade and civilian Auxiliary Fire Service. For meanwhile, although she showed little outward sign of it, the *Maillé-Brézé* was burning furiously and her plight had become more serious with repeated secondary explosions caused by igniting magazines. Archie Sweeney, a relatively new recruit to the AFS, was among the scores of firemen ferried out on 15 drifters, over more than a mile of choppy water, to douse the stricken ship's super-heated structure:

> There was a high wind blowing and it was rather difficult to come alongside her – you could feel the heat from the hull even out in the open air. However, once we'd managed to tie up so many drifters on either side, we got the pumps into operation and very shortly we were pumping thousands of gallons of water a minute into the ship.

Though they were keenly aware of the dangers – not least of more ammunition going up at any time – the firemen selflessly ignored them as they battled on, some of them boarding the vessel and finding the heat from the plates was burning their boot-leather through to the flesh.

In fact the whole exercise was a very high-risk gamble: their actions would either kill the fire (and thus save the ship) or, if the blaze refused to die, they would cause her to sink. For although much of their hosed-on water turned instantly to steam, the more they poured into her, the heavier she got and the greater became the likelihood of her sinking. And as time went on, it seemed the latter result had become a distinct probability. Yet the firemen stuck doggedly to their posts until it was depressingly obvious that they could do no more.

The moment was signalled by the order to abandon ship, issued shortly before eight in the evening. The ship's back was broken, one of her funnels had toppled over, the mizzen mast was sheared; and when her decks became awash, it was clear she could no longer be saved. But just as the disconsolate men clambered off the ship and on to their home-bound vessels, their valour was tested again. Archie Sweeney takes up the story:

> As we were drawing away from the ship, two French petty officers appeared on the scene wearing fire helmets and asking for five men to give them some assistance. The person next to me suggested that we shouldn't be yellow, and he immediately jumped back on the ship. I did likewise, and so did another fireman. So the situation then was that we were standing on the deck of a ship that was going down rather rapidly, and all the drifters had left us, so we were isolated.

Trying not to think about their perilous position, the three volunteers asked what they could do to help and the officers suggested that they try to release the anchor chain – 'presumably to enable the sinking bow to come up, though I wasn't sure that was a good idea' – but even as they made their way towards it, they realised there was no hope: that they were now in very deep trouble, with no means of saving themselves. 'Things were beginning to look rather dangerous,' recalled Archie with considerable understatement. 'The water was rising very rapidly now, and the deck was at quite a severe angle.' Was the three men's bravery about to cost them their lives? Had they volunteered only for a watery grave? It certainly looked like it, but amazingly, at the last moment, their prayers were answered. They could hardly believe their eyes as: 'Suddenly, from nowhere, a little motor-boat with two French sailors on board drew alongside, and they waved to us to jump on board.' Up to their knees in water washing over the big ship's deck, Archie and his mates waded gratefully over to the edge of the deck; but at that critical point one of them suddenly froze on the spot, a non-swimmer unable to make the leap across the swirling vortex of water between the two vessels. 'I was actually the last to leave,' said Archie, 'because in the end I just had to push him off.'Thanking their incredible luck, they breathed again as the motor-boat turned sharply and sped off in a swirl of white water. Behind them, they watched the great ship's head gradually slip under the lapping waves to come to rest on a sandbank, fortuitously clear of both the commercial and naval shipping channels. And as they stepped ashore at Gourock pier in the darkness – it was now about 11 at night – their relief was tempered with a feeling of deep sadness: not because, like all local men, they cared inordinately for ships; but because they knew that still on board the sunken vessel, entombed by layers of twisted metal and freezing depths of water, were the bodies of many men who had not been so lucky as they. And just how many they could not be sure.

In fact, the overall toll at the end of the day the *Maillé-Brézé* sank turned out to be much worse than anyone had expected: 47 hospitalised, six killed outright by the explosion on the upper deck, and no fewer than 28 burned, suffocated or drowned below decks. Their bodies were not recovered until the *Maillé-Brézé* was finally salvaged in 1954, and the sight of them in their last contortions so shocked one of the divers involved that he could no longer take on that kind of work. The bodies of the six sailors who died instantly because they were close to, or working on, the ill-fated torpedo tube, were buried in the shadow of an old evergreen tree in Greenock cemetery soon after the ship's demise, later to be joined by those of three others who did not recover in hospital. And until they were exhumed and returned to France in 1948, their presence served constantly to remind local people not only of the tragic end of the *Maillé-Brézé* but also of the bewildering mystery of it all. They knew, roughly, how it had happened – but why?

Who or what could have caused the release of the exploding torpedo on that awful day of death and destruction? Had battle fatigue among the crewmen caused routine safety precautions to be forgotten or ignored? What about the automatic fail-safe mechanism that should have prevented any torpedo from firing when facing inboard? For the device to have failed in conjunction with momentary carelessness by the relevant maintenance artificer seems a circumstance almost too coincidental to be credible. 'Sabotage' was one of the first words to sweep along the Greenock waterfront almost as soon as the explosion was heard, and despite the wisdom of reflective hindsight and official post-mortems upholding the generally-accepted conclusion that the incident was simply an unfortunate accident, there will always be a nagging suspicion that there was indeed a sinister hand behind the disaster. Because those who were nearest to the incident did not survive to tell their version of the tale, there will always be a variety of theories as to whose hand that might have been.

In the year that the Free French were to succumb to the

invading German armies, there was much suspicion of the pro-German French – soon to become known as Vichyites – and one of the first local conclusions was that a secret sympathiser on board the *Maillé-Brézé* might have quietly arranged for the torpedo to malfunction. Then there were the Nazis themselves. Having failed to knock out the hard-fighting destroyer with their heavy naval hardware at the Battle of Narvik, they might well have reckoned it an easier exercise by far to deliver an audacious fatal blow to her by means of one man's clandestine stealth.

Such imaginative thoughts were refuted dismissively by local naval security officers at the time, who nevertheless managed to add their own dimension of mystery to the matter by pointing out that 'this is a top-secret business'. But whatever the truth was, her destruction was so traumatic and complete that no enemy agent could have done it better. The *Maillé-Brézé* died a no less spectacular death than she would have met in the raging heat of battle, and if the responsibility did indeed rest with one of her own crew, no doubt the enemy indulged in a grim smile of satisfaction at the strange fate of the power-packed destroyer which, ironically, succeeded in destroying herself.

9

A Royal Disaster

ON THE RUGGED, undulating heights near Eagle's Rock, neither David Morrison nor his son Hugh could see the source of it, but the alarmingly close engine noise in the sky above them made the shepherds stop work on rounding-up their sheep and stare up into the densely unrevealing mist. The roar passed overhead, faded slightly, then exploded into a thunder-crack that told them, without doubt, that a large aircraft had come to grief not far away. And there was still more noise. As father and son looked askance at each other, oblivious to their sheep scattering in fright, the grinding, breaking sound seemed to go on and on until it turned into another enormous explosion – which they were to learn later was the noise of 2,500 gallons of aviation fuel blowing up.

It was the early afternoon of Tuesday, 25 August 1942, and news of what they, and a lone angler not far away, had just heard was soon to reverberate all around the world. But the basic, shocking fact that made this accident on a remote Caithness hillside different from hundreds of similar wartime tragedies – if it was indeed an accident – would not become known until the wreckage of the plane, a Royal Air Force Sunderland flying-boat W-4026, was found after many hours of mist-hampered searching by parties from the nearby communities of Dunbeath, Berriedale and Wick. They had been alerted by both the angler and young Hugh Morrison who, after his initial shock, had reacted quickly by sprinting down the hill, jumping on his motor bike, and racing off to raise the alarm.

In some places during their difficult search visibility was down to about 15 feet, and some of the rapidly recruited farmers, gillies and special constables found themselves depending entirely on their sense of smell to lead them to their target. First to find the smouldering wreckage of the plane was farmer James Sutherland. It was a shocking sight – shattered into thousands of pieces, with the bodies of several of its occupants strewn around it. One of them, though still clad in a flying suit, wore a uniform with the ring of an air commodore on the sleeve. His face looked familiar to Sutherland and the friend he had immediately summoned to the location just north of Braemore Falls, shepherd James Gunn (whose son, a schoolboy at the time, later recalled, 'We even caught the smell of the crash at the school, although we didn't know where it was coming from').

Sutherland, Gunn and several other searchers who had now gathered at the spot soon became heroes as, despite their fears about the danger of the burning wreck with its explosive cargo, they decided to approach and search it, one man declaring, 'To hell with bombs, there may be people still alive in there.'

But their own vote for hero of the hour went to the 70-year-old Dr Kennedy from Dunbeath who, after driving about eight miles and traversing another four miles of desolate moorland on foot, turned out to be what a local writer later called 'an industrious and inspiring leader'. Being more accustomed to dealing with death than the others – who were clearly shocked by the carnage and immense scale of the tragedy – he went about the business of checking the bodies inside and outside the plane with calm efficiency, delegating minor duties in a voice of quiet authority. And as he examined the air commodore's body, which had been thrown clear of the wreck, he had to confirm the searchers' initial fears. Although there was a severe gash on the dead man's head, his face was still recognisable to the doctor – who allowed himself a gasp of shock, for the face was that of the 39-year-old George Edward Alexander Edmund, Duke of Kent, youngest brother of the reigning King George VI.

All doubt was dispelled on examination of the dead man's identity bracelet, which was inscribed: *His Royal Highness The Duke of Kent, The Coppins, Iver, Buckinghamshire*. And although it did not seem important at the time, it was noted that his watch had stopped, presumably at the moment of the plane's impact with the ground.

As he concluded his tasks, supervising the covering of the most exposed bodies with their own parachutes, the elderly doctor shook his head with resignation. Although he did not know how many had been aboard the plane, it did appear that they had all perished, a few of them still lying, badly burned, inside the charred fabric of the overturned machine. He had not long reached that conclusion when one of the helpers, police constable Carter from Wick, suddenly exclaimed: 'Listen! I heard a human cry. I'm sure I did!'

The others went quiet and listened hard, but they heard nothing but the sigh of the wind and the call of birds and saw nothing but the rustling heather, even after they had spread out again to make a further search of the immediate area. Putting the alarm down to the policeman's imagination, which could well have been affected by the nerve-racking drama of the day's events, the doctor shook his head sadly again. There was little more he could do now but report to the authorities and help organise removal of the bodies. This arduous task took place the following day, after army personnel were brought in to guard the wreckage and the RAF flew a plane over to establish its precise location. All the bodies were conveyed over difficult terrain to Wick – with the exception of the duke's, which went first to Dunrobin Castle before being removed to London.

A pilot who had risked his life during visits to many bomb-hit British towns, the Duke of Kent was once described by Winston Churchill as 'a gallant and handsome prince'. Known to friends and family affectionately as Georgie, the aircraft-loving duke had a great deal to live for. Only seven weeks before the fatal Iceland-bound flight, he and his wife Marina – the Greek princess to whom he proposed in a lakeside chalet after borrowing the Prince of Wales' plane to fly to Slovenia – had celebrated the birth of their third son, Michael. Just after the birth, they had been visited by Queen Mary, who reported in her diary that 'he looked so happy with his lovely wife and the dear baby'.

Georgie was not only a happy husband and father, he was also delightedly in his element with the role assigned to him in the RAF. Although as a young man he had spent ten years in the Royal Navy – initially based in Scotland, with naval intelligence in Rosyth – now, as Air Commodore, he was directly concerned with the welfare of RAF personnel, reporting to the department of the Inspector General on their living conditions and grievances. Always the most unconventional of the King's brothers, he would often arrive unannounced and unrecognised, perhaps driving his own car, on his visits to home bases. But it was the longer trips he preferred. Loving flying as he did, he most relished his visits to far-flung bases, and indeed his last mission was to be concerned with the welfare of RAF men in Iceland, which had been occupied by the British for over two years.

On the afternoon of 24 August, he said what was to be

his last goodbye to Marina before setting out from London's Euston station on the overnight train to Inverness. The flight's designated departure point was Invergordon, a naval base in the protected inlet of the Cromarty Firth. The Sunderland flying-boat that was to transport him was flown there from its base at Oban, the crew aware only that something special was on. They must have felt honoured to learn, late on the eve of the flight, that they were to be entrusted with such an important passenger. And indeed, they had been hand-picked for the mission.

The pilot, Flight Lieutenant Frank Goyen, was a 25-year-old Australian with an exceptional reputation and nearly a thousand operational hours behind him. Seated beside him as first pilot would be another flyer of long and impressive experience, Wing Commander TL Mosley, Commanding Officer of 228 Squadron. The crew that would back them up were all equally competent and included two more air force pilots – Pilot Officer SW Smith, acting as second officer, and Pilot Officer G R Saunders acting as navigator. The crew numbered ten in all, every one a tried and trusted expert familiar with the rather cumbersome beast that was the Mark III Sunderland with its four Bristol Pegasus Radial engines. Daunting for some perhaps, but surely not for these men, every one of whom valued his life as much as the experience which was the key to his further enjoyment of it. So how could a flight so endowed with professional ability have gone so drastically wrong after only about half-an-hour?

Certainly, the recent mild weather had broken and northern Scotland was blanketed with low cloud, but the waters of the Cromarty Firth were so calm that the Sunderland, carrying a full load of fuel for the long journey and depth-charges in case enemy submarines were spotted en route, had to make an unusually long run before cresting a wave big enough to punch it into the air. With the duke comfortably ensconced in the wardroom in its belly, the heavy plane began to climb at the painfully slow rate of about 200 feet per minute, turning to port to follow the coastline. The idea, presumably, was to round the top of Scotland as much as possible over water, and to avoid short-cutting across the northwest Highlands where some high ground reached over 3,000 feet, presenting an obvious hazard to such a slow-climbing plane. But the most immediate hazard was a frustrating combination of vision-obscuring cloud and mist. Roughly ten minutes into the flight, the skipper was heard to say 'Let's go down and have a look', and the plane descended to keep visual contact with the sea and the coastline on the left. But still more cloud appeared. As clearer weather was expected further north, around the Pentland Firth, some experts have been puzzled as to why the pilot did not simply push on to find it. It has been suggested that perhaps he was just trying to be a good host at this point – wanting to show his royal guest something of the north-east of Scotland – although the duke had probably seen that part of the country before, having only the previous year visited Wick airfield to inspect RAF units there.

Accounts and opinions differ as to what the pilot did next. Considering the catastrophic consequence of whatever it was that influenced his actions, it is often assumed that neither he nor his navigator could have been aware of a westward drift that was bringing the aircraft across the coast and near to inland high ground. Yet it is hard to accept that such a commonly encountered factor in flying would not be acknowledged by a captain and crew of such vast experience, who would be monitoring every move like hawks. Nevertheless, apparently still descending, the plane crossed the coast just south of the

Berriedale Water and, under cloud and mist cover, the high land was coming up to meet it. It flew along the river valley – just avoiding the 2,000-foot summit of Meall Dhonuill, or Donald's Mount, at the end of which was an unwelcome hill rising, at its western extreme, to an almost 1,000-foot-high bluff called Eagle's Rock. Then, as the pilot presumably saw the hill and battled with the controls to find more height – alas, too late – the Sunderland smashed to the ground and burst into the fatal fireball that consumed so many lives. The sensational news of the fate of the duke, the first royal to die on active duty, had an immediate impact not only at home, where public grief was personal and sincere at the loss of such a popular figure, but also abroad. The story was headlined all over the world. Nowhere was it more bitterly accepted than in the heart of his beloved family. Author Christopher Warwick poignantly recounts in his book, *George and Marina,* how those closest to the much-loved Georgie learned of the awful development:

> That evening at Coppins, when the telephone rang, Marina had not long gone to her bedroom, intending to have an early night. Kate Fox, who had nursed the Duchess as a baby [in Greece] 36 years earlier and who had come out of retirement to nurse the now seven-week-old Prince Michael, took the call. Numb with shock, and perhaps wondering just how best to break the news, she slowly climbed the stairs. Hearing her, it is said that Marina immediately sensed catastrophe, and the moment Foxy opened the door, she cried out, 'It's George, isn't it?'
>
> At Balmoral the King and Queen were having dinner with Harry and Alice, the Duke and Duchess of Gloucester, when the steward entered the dining room and whispered

to the King that Sir Archibald Sinclair, Secretary of State for Air, was on the telephone and needed to speak to him urgently. When he rejoined his family, George VI was grim-faced and silent. 'The news,' he wrote, 'came as a great shock to me, & I had to break it to Elizabeth, & Harry & Alice who were staying with us [...] We left Balmoral in the evening for London.'

When the King was called from the table, the Duchess of Gloucester's first thoughts were of Queen Mary – that something had happened to her. In fact the Queen Dowager had spent the day in active high spirits. During the morning she had driven over to Corsham Court, home of Lord Methuen, to attend a lecture and admire the picture gallery; had spent the rest of that wet afternoon at Badminton, putting photographs into her huge scarlet folio albums; and after tea had sat at needlework, while Lady Cynthia Colville, one of her ladies-in-waiting, read to her. News of Georgie's death was received shortly after dinner. 'I felt so stunned by the shock,' Queen Mary wrote in her diary, 'I could not believe it.' The following morning the Queen climbed into her famous old Daimler and drove to Coppins. When she arrived, she found Marina in a pitifully desolate state; one moment sobbing uncontrollably, the next staring blankly into space, utterly motionless.

There was to be still more drama on the remote Scottish hillsides. From the body count (there should have been 15) it appeared that one person was still missing. And indeed, 22 hours after the crash, came the evidence that vindicated the 'imaginative' constable Carter's keen hearing. One man, 21-year-old rear gunner Andrew Jack, had miraculously survived the crash, as the tail turret of the Mark III Sunderland – normally considered the most vulnerable part of such a plane – had broken off almost intact. The next day, he dramatically appeared three miles from the scene, barefooted and dazed, his clothes in shreds, badly burned about the face and body, at a lonely cottage where he just managed to say: 'I am an airman and our plane has crashed. I am the sole survivor.'

How did he know that was the case? Despite his injuries, he had searched the wreckage vainly for other survivors before staggering off towards the merciful refuge of the cottage. He was looked after there until the arrival of Dr Kennedy who, passing that way only by chance, was amazed not only to find a survivor from the devastated plane but also to realise that the young man had managed to walk so far over rough ground in such a bad condition. Quickly removed to hospital in Lybster, the fortunate flight-sergeant made a good recovery.

Though he did recall a few details of the fateful flight – such as the skipper Goyen's suggestion that they 'go down and have a look' – this lucky son of a Grangemouth dock foreman was never to be properly valued as the key witness in the affair. Possibly because, despite an official inquiry, the affair itself was oddly played down for many years. Although it did eventually become a much-talked-about mystery, the renewed interest came too late in the day – Andrew Jack died in 1978, before questions began to be asked in earnest, but not before he had told his sister that he could never agree with the inquiry's finding that the crash had been caused by pilot error. Certainly, in the time-honoured tradition of all blame for such an accident being shouldered by the captain, the inquiry had not been disposed to give Flight Lieutenant Goyen much benefit of the doubt.

Sir Archibald Sinclair reported to the Commons on 7

October, 1942, that the court of inquiry had found:

> First, that the accident occurred because the aircraft was flown on a track other than that indicated in the flight plan given to the pilot, and at too low an altitude to clear the rising ground on the track; secondly, that the responsibility for this serious mistake in airmanship lies with the captain of the aircraft; thirdly, that the weather encountered should have presented no difficulties to an experienced pilot; fourthly, that the examination of the propellers showed that the engines were under power when the aircraft struck the ground, and fifthly, that all the occupants of the aircraft were on duty at the time of the accident.

If the aircraft had flown on a track 'other than that indicated in the flight plan' – and there were several ways of getting from Invergordon to Reykjavik – how can that be checked today? Where is the flight plan now? It has apparently disappeared. Just one of many oddities discovered when, in the early 1980s, Edinburgh writer and broadcaster Robin McWhirter decided to take up all the loose strings of the affair and try to tie them together. He quickly realised he was walking a path 'littered with inaccuracies' and found himself asking many key questions to which he could get no official answers. Why did the record book of 228 Squadron, Coastal Command, to which the flying-boat belonged, record 2pm as the time of the crash when the plane took off a 1.10pm and could not have been flying for much more than 30 minutes? (The plane's clock had stopped at 1.30pm, while the time shown on the duke's stopped watch was said to have indicated that the flight had lasted 32 minutes). Why did *Hansard* record the date of the crash as 15 August, when the true date was ten days later?

Why has all documentation pertaining to the official court of inquiry disappeared? Why do the Public Record Office, the RAF's Air Historical Branch and the Royal Archives at Windsor Castle all deny having the vital records relating to the death of the man who was fifth in line to the throne when he died? Why did the Queen's private secretary and keeper of the Windsor Archives state that he was 'not permitted to release the very few other documents which are of relevance'? Why, on the very day of the fatal flight, did pilot Goyan give Andrew Jack a signed photo of himself bearing the written message 'With memories of happier days'? Did the skipper perhaps know something that made him feel apprehensive about the forthcoming Iceland trip? A trip, incidentally, that Jack had made several times.

Accepting that pilot error might not have been the cause, could there have been some sinister hand behind the apparent accident that had done considerable damage to British public morale? Not to put too fine a point on it: had an enemy agent tampered with the plane? There appeared to be no evidence and no way of proving such a thing but, paradoxically perhaps, in Lisbon of all places there was something a little more definite to support a theory of home-grown sabotage. In fact, recalled McWhirter, the German ambassador to Portugal, Baron Oswald von Hoyningen-Huene, had sent the following telegram to the German Foreign Minister Joachim von Ribbentrop on 5 December 1942:

As the embassy has learned, confidentially, the death of the Duke of Kent has been discussed recently in the inner-most circles of the British Club here. The gist of the talk being that an act of sabotage was involved. It is said that the duke, like the Duke of Windsor, was sympathetic towards an understanding with Germany and so gradually had become a problem for the Government clique. The people who were accompanying him were supposed to have expressed themselves along similar lines, so that getting them out of the way would also have been an advantage.

McWhirter was, however, unable to find any evidence to support this rather far-fetched contention and concluded that 'the British community in Lisbon was misinformed about those accompanying the Duke of Kent'.

Among the plethora of more technical, and less romantic, theories for the cause of the crash put forward by various writers and experts over the years have been the disorientating influence of magnetic rocks on the aircraft's compass (Ralph Barker: *Great Mysteries of the Air*) and the effect of downdraught on its altitude (Francis Thompson: *Murder and Mystery in the Highlands*). But it also has to be said that skipper Goyen, although thought by many to have been unjustly maligned with the official pilot-error verdict, did not exactly receive the unqualified support of the RAF pilot who came along the next day to check the position of the wreckage from the air. This was the late Captain EE Fresson whose son Richard submitted the story of his flight for publication in letters page of *The Scotsman* in September 1985, after that newspaper had published McWhirter's searching questions on the affair. The pilot's log, as it was called, began on the same day as the crash:

> I happened to be on the Inverness–Kirkwall run that day and the Met Office reported bad weather along the route as far as the Pentland Firth, where conditions improved.
>
> We flew north above the cloud at 4,000 feet and found

121

the Pentland Firth bathed in sunshine with the sea looking a deep emerald green. We departed from Kirkwall around one o'clock in the afternoon on the return trip and flew around the west side of Hoy across to Thurso in sunny weather. We caught up with the low cloud again at Thurso, when I turned off on the south-easterly course to bring the plane over Dunbeath on the Caithness coastline and which we passed over above cloud at 1.30pm. At approximately the same time as we departed from Kirkwall, the [duke's] Sunderland flying-boat took off from the Cromarty Firth... climbed above the clouds and set course for the west side of Hoy, before changing course for the overseas flight to Reykjavik.

For some unknown reason, after being airborne for barely ten minutes, the captain was heard by the rear gunner over the intercom to say, 'Let's go down and have a look'. Knowing as he must have done that there was a very low ceiling on the first part of the trip, I never understood what possessed that captain to take such unnecessary risks. He only had to fly on course for another ten minutes and he would have had the whole of the Pentland Firth in view.

However, down they went and at about 200 feet they broke cloud to find themselves in a narrow valley, running parallel to the coastline, north of the small village of Berriedale. That valley extends roughly three miles northwards and at the end, the ground rises sharply up from near sea level to a thousand feet. With the poor visibility, the pilot evidently failed to see the sharply-rising ground in time. The aircraft clock found in the wreckage had stopped at half-past one, the time I was actually flying overhead and changing course for Inverness.

On the morning of August 26, I was informed through

RAF Fighter Control at Drumossie about the accident. As the whereabouts of the wreckage was not accurately known, we were asked to keep a look-out on our flights north. I set out on a flight to North Ronaldsay via Kirkwall and I made for the Dunbeath area flying inland a few miles up the coast from Berriedale and over the same small valley where the Sunderland had evidently descended.

Suddenly we came on the wreckage at the top of the escarpment, strewn over a large area. The aircraft had evidently caught fire for the wreckage was still smoking. The fragmentation had evidently been severe. I descended to 100 feet and flew around. The four engines were scattered around the wreckage. The only recognisable part of the sea-plane was the rear gun-turret, rudder and tail-fin which had evidently broken away from the structure at the point of impact.

My radio officer and I could distinguish three or four bodies lying amongst the debris. It was obvious that the considerable amount of fuel on board had caught fire and had melted much of the light alloy wreckage. The position of the crash was some eight miles southwest of the village of Dunbeath and the altitude was around eight to nine hundred feet above sea level. The aircraft must have crashed in cloud.

After climbing to 2,000 feet to obtain strong radio signals with Inverness, my radio officer tapped out a message to Inverness Control informing them that we had located the Sunderland and that, as far as we could tell, there were no survivors.

Three weeks after the disaster, on 14 September, King George VI drove from Balmoral to Berriedale, then made his way on foot towards the location of his brother's death. His party, which included the Duke of Sutherland, the chief constable of the county and several RAF officers, was led across the difficult terrain by a local gamekeeper, James Macewan, who had received the alarmed angler on the day of the crash and passed on his alert to police headquarters at Wick.

The king was also introduced to many of the other key players in the drama, including the shepherds David and Hugh Morrison and Dr Kennedy, who, as the searchers' spokesman, recounted to him the grim details of their discovery of the wreckage and bodies. And although the wreckage had by now been removed from the site, the royal guest was clearly moved by what evidence of the disaster remained to be seen. He later described his visit there as a 'pilgrimage' and wrote that 'the ground for 200 yds long & 100 yds wide had been scored and scorched by its trail & by flame. It hit one side of the slope, turned over in the air & slid down the other side on its back. The impact must have been terrific as the aircraft as an aircraft was unrecognisable when found'.

The heartbroken Marina could not bring herself to visit the site until several years later, and, perhaps thankfully, nature had by then done its healing work and there was little left to see of the path of devastation the king had described. Today, the spot is marked by a tall, simple cross atop a granite plinth bearing the names of those who died, the only physical reminder of an unexplained tragedy whose cause, it seems, will be forever argued about.

Just as it was when McWhirter raised the subject in his *Scotsman* article timed to coincide with his 1985 radio programme, *The Crash of W-4026*. It did not just prompt the appearance of Captain Fresson's account. The paper's letters page bubbled with theories, opinions and observations of varying quality, as the revitalised controversy took on an unprecedented intensity. Arguments between letter-writers bounced back and forth. Calculators were drawn. Rates of climb, distances and headings flown, the condition of the plane's instruments, the quality of the skipper's briefing, the time of the impact, the likelihood of sabotage, and even the possibility of the crew's performance being impaired by alcohol: all were gone into in the greatest of detail by expert and amateur alike. But in the end it seemed the baffled reader could reach only one conclusion: that precisely why the Duke of Kent's flying-boat had crashed remained a perplexing mystery, ever more unfathomable the more one considered the expertise and qualities of its crew.

One writer pointed out that such a crash was anything but rare during the war; that as many as 80 Sunderlands had been destroyed in and around Scotland, only two of them put down by enemy action. And 15 similar accidents had occurred in the area of the duke's crash, 12 of them being fatal with a total of 77 lives lost. 'Hardly any of these,' wrote Malcolm Spaven, 'were attributed to technical causes; most were due directly to pilot or navigator error, leading to aircraft becoming hopelessly lost in cloud and flying into hills.'

What McWhirter would not yield to, however, was any suggestion that echoed the official inquiry's conclusion of 'a serious mistake in airmanship' being to blame. Having, in his original article, stressed the extreme unlikelihood of skipper Goyen making such an elementary error as failing to seek altitude in bad visibility, he countered with emphatic and final conviction:

Frank Goyen was a cool, sober pilot with all six senses ticking over. That was why he and his crews survived so long among the dreadful statistics which Malcolm Spaven has listed. There is much more I could write about the crew of W-4026, but I will limit myself to one sentence. Whatever caused the tragedy at Eagle's Rock, it wasn't pilot error.

10

A Scream in the Night

SHRIEKING GULLS WHEEL and glide in the bitter winds
that sweep across the shoreline and power the huge waves
that crash across the harbour mouth's protective piers like
cascading fireworks. Elemental forces are still impressively at
work around Aberdeen's ancient entrance from the North Sea
where, on a chill December morning in 1945, Betty Hadden's
severed left forearm was found washed up by such waves
among the seaweed-coated stones on the south shore of the
harbour's narrow navigation channel.

Today, the post-oil-boom but still colourful port vicinity is
a less sinister place than it was in Betty Hadden's day, when
the piratical vestiges of an older fishing and seafaring culture
lingered on among the dockside bars and cafes in a network of
seedy streets where now there are modern offices and service
depots.

For glamour-seeking Betty, the seductive old harbour area
of Torry had a magnetic and masculine attraction, at a time
of life when conventional entertainment wasn't enough: she
would have been 18 years old if she had lived a few more
days. But her restless nature wouldn't wait for anything. Her
city wasn't exactly boring: it had plenty of dance-halls and
picture houses where a girl could get a second-hand taste of
Hollywood glamour – 19 cinemas, in fact; more than any
other comparable British city. But Betty, who had a variety
of menial jobs behind her – waitress in a dockside cafe, fish
gutter, domestic servant, mill-hand – was more tempted by the

first-hand escapism of real money and real excitement. And it seemed that the little brunette with the turned-down mouth and sulky eyes had discovered how to find it. A discovery that was to prove literally fatal.

But who killed Betty Hadden? In the beginning, it seemed that this elementary question would be quickly answered as the police made what the local press described as 'a brilliant start' to their enquiries on the case. For the most immediate mystery – to whom did the gruesome human remains found on the foreshore belong? – was solved within four hours. Yet, despite their flying start and prodigious and persistent follow-up efforts to run the killer to ground, to this day he or she remains a 'person unknown'.

The first indication that something dreadful might have happened to a woman came with a scream that pierced through the early morning darkness of 12 December. It rang out over the harbour area at around 2am and awakened many nearby people who, not entirely unaccustomed to late night revelry and drunken disputes around Torry's quayside pubs, turned over in their beds and thought little more about it... until press coverage and police enquiries sharpened their recall. Had that scream come from the throat of Betty Hadden as she struggled with her murderer? Nobody could ever be certain, but it seemed to fit in well with the sequence of events The second alarm, more shocking by far, was to come from the same area only about seven hours later that day.

While the cold Granite City started to get into its stride for what it assumed would be just another working Wednesday – shops opening, trams clanking up and down Union Street, heavy horses and square-topped vans criss-crossing the thoroughfares to make deliveries – old Alexander King was also up and about on his habitual morning pursuit: searching for driftwood on the south foreshore of the navigational channel, overlooked by a steep grassy embankment. When he saw the gleaming white object lying among the seaweedy pebbles and rocks, he stepped back warily, then gathered his courage to approach it again. Peering down to examine it, he gasped as he realised the object was a human forearm with the hand still attached and the fingers arched as if they had been scratching at something or someone. There was a length of twine granny-knotted around the wrist. Shocked and trembling, the 74-year-old retired cooper suddenly found some reserves of youthful energy as he hurried back up to the channel-side road, to call the police from the nearest telephone box.

First reactions to news of the discovery had a touch of battle weariness about them. The war was just over, during which people had become accustomed to death and destruction, and this seemed like something similarly impersonal: the grisly relic, perhaps, of some distant sea battle or disaster. But when Detective Superintendent John Westland, who was to lead the investigation, went to the mortuary to see the evidence for himself, he realised not only that it was rather too fresh for a wartime relic but also that there was something odd about it that required an expert eye.

He called in police surgeon Dr Robert Richards – who, after a preliminary examination, announced that it was the forearm of a young woman 'about 18 years old' who had been alive less than three days before. But it was his expert view on how it had been severed from the body that alerted police to the fact that this might not have been by accident. He shrugged aside colleagues' suggestions that the woman might simply have been drowned at sea, her body dismembered by the propeller of a passing ship, and was emphatic about his own conclusion: that the arm had been deliberately cut off at the elbow, probably with a knife or a saw, or both.

All those present at this macabre scene looked at each other in the grim realisation that what they were dealing with was evidence of a particularly calculated and cold-blooded murder. And as the arm was being routinely photographed, before being taken away for further examination to the forensic laboratories at Aberdeen University, Superintendent Westland issued an order which, he thought then, was based on only a slender and optimistic hope of quick identification: 'It should be fingerprinted as well, of course.'

His instinct was right. It signalled the 'brilliant start' acknowledged in the press. Already an entry in police files, the name Betty Hadden was found to match the prints from the arched, nicotine-stained fingers within a matter of hours. And a young detective received something of a shock when – as he had been looking for a girl of that name in connection with a minor offence at the old Castlehill Barracks – a laboratory colleague with a black sense of humour came to him, produced the forearm, and said: 'You wanted Betty Hadden, didn't you? Well, there you are!'

The police launched a massive dragnet operation in the hope of making an equally quick arrest. Armed with long, probing 'graips' and working with small boats, wellington-booted officers turned over tons of tangle and flotsam as they scoured the boulder-strewn estuary for the rest of the body. Every ship in the harbour was checked from stem to stern and all those which had left in the previous few days were boarded by police at their next port of call. In a street-by-street comb-out of two square miles of the Torry district, officers spent hours of unpaid overtime going in and out of local houses removing wash-hand basins for forensic examination, through back gardens, down sewers, across waste ground, and into cellars, wash-houses and sheds, collecting every sample of blood they came across. There was ox blood, fish blood, and even a dead pig became involved, but there was no human match to Betty Hadden.

A pig? To work out where the arm had originally entered the water, weather scientists from Aberdeen University were enlisted to cooperate with a special group of detectives assigned to the case. One of those detectives was John Nicol, who recalled some years later how 'the foreleg of a pig, representing the arm, was put into the water to test where the current would take it, and the winds and tides provided the answer'. Which was? The very point where the arm had been found! Clearly, if the murder had not actually been committed in the Torry district, disposal of at least part of it had taken place there. But from a ship or from dry land? That was only one of the vital questions which teased and challenged the police; but to which even speculative answers proved stubbornly elusive.

With their frustration growing rapidly, and ship checks proving fruitless, they appealed to residents of the district, and motorists who had passed through it, to come forward with information about anything unusual they had seen or heard on the night Betty was thought to have died: thus the 'scream in the night' stories. 'With the help of a volunteer policewoman, we even re-enacted the scene of a woman screaming down by the old Torry pier in the dead of night,' recalled Nicol, who later became an assistant chief constable of Grampian police. It helped, but only to strengthen the assumption of the time of the girl's death.

Meanwhile, Betty's mother, the widow of a shipyard worker, spoke uneasily about her daughter's life. 'She worked in fish yards, but in her last two places she stayed only about three days.' Kate Hadden had not seen her daughter for nearly two weeks before her death, adding that Betty had stayed away from home before. Police began to build up a picture of the girl's aimless waterfront life: working here, working there, sleeping in unimaginable places, mixing with strangers by day and by night. They could not prove that the scream in the night was the last that was ever heard of her – or even that she died on that day, at that time – but they did manage to create a relatively reliable diary of late sightings of her.

On the previous Monday, she was seen in the company of four girls opposite the town house. On the same night, she was spotted in Castle Street, walking arm-in-arm with two young naval ratings, one much taller than the other. The next day, she was seen in the Torry area and later leaning against the wall of a city centre shop, 'eating buns and biscuits hungrily'; then back in the harbour area, 'trying to attract the attention of three sailors'.

She was never seen alive again. Try as they might, the police made no progress in the search for her killer, presumed to be a man – if only because of the butcher's technique that had been used to sever the arm.

Paul Harris, an Aberdonian author who has studied the case, voices one popular local view about Betty Hadden's fate when he says:

> I tend to go along with the school of thought that says she was simply picked up by some visiting sailors who had their way with her, perhaps over violently, perhaps causing injury, then – suddenly afraid of repercussions – decided to shut her up for good by throwing her overboard in pieces to be fed to the fish.

Despite a relatively short time in the water, the back of the hand had been partially eaten by crabs. The twine around the wrist had been bound so loosely that it seemed there might have been a loop to it, inside which some kind of weight might had been placed, later accidentally slipping out. Along with various other pieces of potential evidence from the shore area of the arm's discovery – scraps of cloth, metal, and other materials – the twine was sent to the police laboratory at Nottingham for detailed examination by Dr HS Holden, an eminent forensic criminologist. It was found to be common binder twine of the kind used by tradesmen, farmers and shopkeepers, and yielded no new leads.

The arm, meanwhile, was taking on something of a life of its own. More experts had been called in to examine it, notably Professor Sydney Smith of Edinburgh University whose opinion, as one of Britain's foremost figures in forensic medicine, was highly valued – and backed up that of police surgeon Richards. The professor agreed with him that both a saw and a knife had almost certainly been used to dismember the arm and said that the size of the saw, and the pressure put on it, could be determined from the marks it made on the bone and from the point at which the last splinter broke off. Sir John Learmonth, another eminent authority (on the amputation of limbs), reported that by carefully reconstructing the body's dismemberment, he could establish the position it was lying in when the 'operation' took place.

As time passed and police progress ground to a dispiriting halt, the limb became something of a celebrated object in the history of Scottish criminology. With the intention of preserving it for posterity, Professor RD Lockhart had it bottled, labelled and shelved in his anatomy department at Aberdeen University, and, thus packaged, it even made a macabre appearance – to the distress of some of the bow-tied guests – during a talk at the university given by Superintendent Westland. But several years after the anatomy professor's retirement, the arm was impulsively disposed of in a general clean-out of the department, a move which surprised many people, not least the professor himself.

'I am very sorry to learn that it has not been kept,' he told the press when he heard the news. 'If I had thought there was a possibility they were not going to look after it, I would have brought it down to the Museum of Anthropology, where I am now curator.'

So, ignominiously, vanished the last trace of Betty Hadden, leaving two perplexing mysteries: Where was the rest of her corpse? And who was her murderer? It is disturbing to think that he might be walking free in some far-off corner of the globe – or still living in the neighbourhood of Torry. 'Until his dying day,' said John Nicol, 'it remained a bitter disappointment to Superintendent Westland that the killer was never brought to justice and the case cleared up.'

Police appeals to the public did not bring forward Jack Webster, who was a schoolboy at the time. Now an author, he has written about the case, asking if he might have been able to help police to trace the murderer.

In his early fascination with newspapers and avid study of their treatment of such sensational tales, he remembers being riveted to the story unfolding in the *Aberdeen Evening Express*. One report said Betty Hadden had close friends in the Froghall district, and another line that a youth had been known to carry messages to her there. 'I knew I was not that youth,' he wrote in his autobiography, *A Grain of Truth,* 'though the description was similar; but from the hazy recollection of the name on the envelope, I had carried a note to someone who could have been Betty Hadden or a friend of hers who had an address in Froghall. The police were anxious to trace sailors and I had a clear picture of the one [who had given him the note] at Holburn Junction.'

How had this come about?

At the corner of Holburn Junction, my friend Alastair Crombie and I were distracted by a call from a doorway. It was a sailor asking if we would care to earn a couple of bob by delivering a message. We would have to take a letter to a certain house, wait to see if there was a reply, and bring it back to the same place at a given time. Swayed by the prospect of earning two bob instead of spending it, we agreed and set out for a district which had a mixed reputation: Froghall. It was a slum-clearance district, it seemed, but even then deteriorating into the sort of condition from which the inhabitants had so recently moved. We climbed the communal staircase, gripped by a sleazy excitement in this rather sinister setting... Nervously, we knocked on the door which was opened by a woman of brittle appearance who took the letter and disappeared inside. From the doorway, a couple of 14-year-olds, slightly apprehensive, could see and hear the revelry of a carefree household. The war was over and it was pub-closing time as drunken servicemen lolled in chairs with women on their knees, exposing legs and thighs and goodness knows what. The woman who took the note returned to say that there would be no reply, so we left and hurried back to Holburn Junction for the appointed hour. The sailor, a smallish, dark, stocky fellow, was already there waiting. We gave him the news and never saw him again...

Could that have been a significant incident? Jack admits he just doesn't know, 'but Alastair and I sat on our secret, nervously protecting ourselves with silence [to avoid the risk of severe discipline at school]... a silence maintained while sailors on boats were followed to the ends of the earth.'

Certainly, as recalled by John Nicol, there was a chance that a sailor was the culprit 'but we got no results after checking all ships which had sailed from Aberdeen'. He preferred to believe, in any case, that the killer was a local man. 'A man in Torry was our chief suspect, but we did not have enough evidence against him.'

Despite Paul Harris's feeling that Hadden was thrown overboard from a visiting ship, other writers speculating about the case seem to have agreed with Nicol, forming a consensus that the killer lived locally. Webster himself claims:

> The killer of Betty Hadden had probably disposed of the body in a trunk but was unable to tuck in the surplus arm. So he sawed it off and carelessly disposed of it in the river. There were those who believed that the murderer was a local person who knew the lie of the land, a quiet inhabitant of Torry who continued perhaps to live out his life with an air of respectability.

And Peter Piper wrote in the *Scottish Sunday Express*:

> Betty Hadden, shiftless and haphazard as she was, was not a 'pick-up girl' in the accepted sense of that phrase. I feel convinced that on the night of December 11 she met someone ruthless and brutal and savage enough to attempt by force to overcome her. She fought against this man and died. And I believe, too, that this man lived in Torry

or nearby, or at least had access to some building there where he dismembered the body.

All of which gives rise to an uncomfortable thought. If Betty Hadden's body had indeed been squashed into a trunk, and if her killer was indeed a local man, where is that trunk now? Was it also consigned to the deep? If not, it seems inconceivable that the murderer, presumably shocked by the boomerang-like return of the once-weighted arm, would have taken another similar – and even greater – risk by returning to the water to dispose of the trunk and the butchered body. The idea is undoubtedly a ghastly one, but no less ghastly than the whole macabre tale itself: could the unrecovered remains yet be found, buried under the lawn of a respectable back garden in the vicinity of the waterfront world where Betty met her untimely, nightmarish death?

Time might ultimately tell; and then again, it probably won't.

11

Blood Money

APART FROM THE howling of the chill North Atlantic winds that sweep across its bleak, treeless moors, it is normally a very quiet place, the island of Lewis. Survival and social interdependence being high priorities for its hardy people who have quite enough trouble from the elements, there is little time for hostility among neighbours. A murder is thus a very rare occurrence in their far-flung northwestern fastness and when it happens, it is met with shock and disbelief. In fact, there have been only two in living memory – in 1938, when an islander was charged with killing his wife but escaped execution by being certified insane; and in 1968, when the close-knit island community was appalled at the brutal murder of an old woman in the tiny west coast village of Brue, in Barvas parish about 12 miles from Stornoway.

Who was responsible for the second murder? That is the mystery that has bewildered many islanders since a young weaver walked free from the High Court at Inverness three months after the discovery of 80-year-old Mary Mackenzie's body on a mid-November morning. A neighbour, crofter Angus Maclean, had become suspicious when he noticed that her bedroom curtains, normally drawn and pinned only at the bottom to form a V-shape because she was too small to reach up further, were completely closed. Finding the kitchen door unlocked, he entered the old lady's little house and called out her name repeatedly. There was no response, so he ventured into the bedroom to be confronted by a macabre scene.

Surrounded by pieces of torn newspaper – it was generally known that the rather eccentric old lady kept considerable sums of money wrapped up in bundles of such paper – Miss Mackenzie was lying on the floor in a pool of blood. Her nightdress and stockings were bloodstained, there were lacerations on her head, and her hands were folded across her breast. It appeared that her feet had been moved, describing an arc in the blood. And a broken alarm clock was found beside her, with its hands stopped at 5.55. However, Mr Maclean knew that one of her odd habits was to keep the clock running two hours fast.

At 9.15 the following Tuesday night, CID officers led by Detective Superintendent Robert Brown of Glasgow, entered the nearby home of 21-year-old weaver George Macleod and arrested him. Charged with murder at Stornoway Sheriff Court, he was taken to the airport by police officers to board the flight for Inverness where he was to be held at Porterfield Prison until his High Court trial. That was when the shock that had kept the island talking since the body's discovery turned into stunned disbelief. Macleod was one of a respectable family of four sons and three daughters who, living less than a hundred yards from Mary Mackenzie's house, knew the old lady well. In the same court where he was accused of striking her repeatedly on the head with an unknown instrument and robbing her of a sum of money unknown – and a handkerchief – he was also described by witnesses as 'a quiet lad' and 'a likeable and well-behaved boy'. His father Donald characterised him in the witness stand as 'a good-hearted fellow'.

When the complicated five-and-a-half day trial got under way before the Lord Justice Clerk, Lord Grant, the apparent shattering of the innocence of island life captured the public imagination: there were queues of people lining up for the sessions, and on the last day as many as 200 were turned away.

But if they had hoped to hear evidence that would inject clarity and definition into the case, they were to be disappointed. What they heard was a confusing chain of circumstantial facts and scenarios that could be broken, claimed the defence, 'link by link'. Paradoxically, it was perhaps an indication of the inherent weakness of the Crown's case that there were no fewer than 80 prosecution witnesses cited to appear, while only six were scheduled to be put forward by the defence, led by Lionel Daiches QC, the formidable advocate once described by writer and broadcaster Colin Bell as

> the undisputed master of the final speech to the jury, the extravagant display of learning, wit and language which can occasionally acquit a man in the teeth of all the evidence [and] in whose hands a minor discrepancy in the evidence becomes a monstrous chasm of injustice through which the Crown will pass only at our peril.

As the trial went on, before a jury of seven men and eight women, it began to look like a classic case for the Daiches treatment. While conceding that the evidence against Macleod was largely circumstantial, Advocate Depute John McCluskey QC sought, through witnesses, to demonstrate that all the elements added up to the sum of guilty.

It appeared that the murder – the obvious motive for which was robbery – had taken place in the early hours of Friday 15 November. Dr Ian Murray said he examined Miss Mackenzie, who had been his patient, at about noon that day and estimated that she had died between 6 and 12 hours earlier, after being bludgeoned by an instrument that was 'not very sharp or very heavy... it would have had an edge of some kind, but not a sharp edge'. And Dr Edgar Rentoul, a Glasgow University lecturer in forensic medicine who carried out a post-mortem on the body, said she died from multiple lacerations of the scalp, fractures of the skull, and concussion. In his opinion, the 'cruel and savage' attack was probably carried out with a blunt object 'such as an iron bar, a stone, or even a boot'. There was talk of a crowbar that had been seen in the possession of Macleod's friend Donald Matheson around the time of the murder, and it was produced as an exhibit in court. But in reply to Mr Daiches, Matheson claimed the crowbar had remained in a cupboard at his home on the night of 14 November and all the following day.

Dolina MacDonald, a neighbour of both Macleod and the murdered woman, told the court she had been disturbed around the presumed time of the killing by a knock on her window – and the voice of Macleod calling her name. She called out: 'What are you doing here at this time of night?' And they exchanged comments about the time. She said it was two in the morning, and as she saw him illuminate his watch with the aid of a burning cigarette, he claimed it was going on for midnight. 'I told him to go home and he said he was sorry.' When, after learning of Miss Mackenzie's murder, she saw spots of blood on the window, she reported the incident to the police. But when Daiches pointed out that forensic scientists had established that the blood on the window was that of a hen, she responded: 'Yes, I know that now.'

Detective Inspector James Junor read a statement given by Macleod during an interview at Stornoway police station, in which the accused claimed he had been drinking with friends until 1.30 on the morning in question and then 'went straight home. I was not near any other place that night. I haven't been in old Mary's house for a month'.

But then there was the small matter of the suitcase found

in his house...

At the police station, Macleod had been invited to unlock it, and he did so with a key on a ring taken from his pocket. The case contained a number of items, including a handkerchief and £45 in an envelope. This money, it was alleged, included 23 single £1 notes of the British Linen Bank, seven of them bearing the serial number *T/4*. Earlier, it had been stated that £100 in new British Linen notes of the *T/4* series had been issued to old age pensioners in the area, whereas the accused was paid for his weaving work in notes of the Bank of Scotland and Bank of England. And PC John Fraser, questioned by Mr McCluskey, agreed that his inquiries among a cross-section of the community, in search of British Linen Bank notes bearing that serial number, had been less than successful.

The jury also heard that a National Commercial Bank £1 note allegedly found in the suitcase had a piece missing from it, and two pieces of a banknote found at the dead woman's home had, according to the police, fitted the gap perfectly. The joining-up of the jigsaw was demonstrated to the jury with a series of photographs, but Daiches tackled this challenging exercise laterally. 'Was there anything found on Macleod or his clothing to indicate that he had been in that house?' he asked the first policeman delivering this evidence. He replied, 'As far as I am aware, no, sir.' And from the policeman in charge of the photographs – Detective Inspector Osborne Butler, of the Identification Bureau, City of Glasgow Police – the admission was extracted that he had been unable to find one single, whole, identifiable fingerprint there. A strand of hair found clutched in Miss Mackenzie's hand had promised to be an important clue, but on examination it had not come from George Macleod and was similar in texture and colour to her own. One of the key planks of the prosecution's case was George

Macleod's apparently urgent need for money. Social Security inspector Alistair Mackenzie pointed out that, while in the two previous years Macleod had sent in his National Insurance stamp card to them after only one reminder, for the year in question he had needed two reminders. And clerical officer Mary Morrison said that the sum of £47 19s due on 15 November was all paid in single notes.

The Advocate Depute saw this 'sudden acquisition of wealth' on the morning after Miss Mackenzie's death as 'significant'. And in his closing speech, he also pointed out not only that robbery had been the only possible motive for the crime but that the old lady's assailant must have been someone she knew and recognised.

In Macleod's defence, however, Daiches pointed out that he had no record of violence and suggested that the wrong man had been charged. He said the prosecution's deductions made 'a chain strung out by fibres of the imagination which could be blown away by a breath of air'. There was nothing to connect George Macleod with the murder house or the murder itself. He referred to several of the items of evidence on which the prosecution case depended – the crowbar, the hair clutched in the victim's hand, the handkerchief, the hen's blood on the neighbour's window – and asserted that none of them had ultimately anything to do with the case. 'As one looks at the Crown case, one sees it melting away before one's eyes,' he said. 'It doesn't add up.'

Caution was the judge's watchword. In his summing-up to the jury, which lasted one-and-a-half hours, Lord Grant warned of the dangers of speculation and suspicion, reminding them of the circumstantial nature of the Crown evidence. Had guilt beyond reasonable doubt been established? The onus on the Crown to prove this was a heavy one. The questions of robbery and murder in the case were very much interrelated. If it had not been ascertained that Macleod had robbed Miss Mackenzie, the jury could not bring a guilty verdict. The question for its members was whether the evidence as a whole established guilt... and unless Macleod was guilty of the whole charge, he was not guilty at all.

Eighty minutes of tension followed – later described by George Macleod as 'the longest wait I have had in my life' – then, as the jury returned to announce its unanimous 'not proven' verdict, spontaneous applause broke out in the packed public gallery. Macleod himself took the news quietly and calmly, but more applause filled the courtroom as Lord Grant discharged the young weaver. Twice, a court official had to rise and shout for silence as the longest trial of its kind to be held in Inverness came to an undignified close.

Outside the courtroom, surrounded by back-slapping friends and relatives congratulating him in Gaelic, a relieved Macleod told reporters about the 'terrible strain' he had been under:

> I was feeling weak sometimes during the trial, knowing that I had nothing to do with it and yet people were coming out with evidence against me. I was wondering why on earth all this was happening to me when I had nothing to do with it.'

He revealed that, on the Saturday night after Miss Mackenzie's death, he had attended a wake for her in the village.

> I was feeling terrible to hear about her death, and it was even more terrible to be charged with her murder after having been at her wake.

'Not proven' being a uniquely Scottish verdict that lacks the definite, thoroughly cleansing conclusion of 'not guilty', he was asked if he felt completely satisfied with the jury's decision. 'I'm not worried about the verdict,' he said, 'so long as I'm free... I'm feeling fine now and I'm going back to the weaving.'

Simultaneously, back in Brue – across the road from where Miss Mackenzie lived – his mother broke down and wept when she heard the jury's decision. 'This is wonderful news,' she said. 'It is a tremendous relief to us all and an answer to our prayers. I am glad it is all over... George is still a young lad and I hope he will soon get over this terrible experience.'

So who was the killer of Mary Mackenzie? One of Lionel Daiches's witnesses, who was dubbed the Red Herring, obviously had suspicions about a dark stranger who appeared in Barvas on the night of the murder – but, as the evidence had no direct relevance to the Macleod case, the matter was passed over without further development. Nevertheless, to garage proprietor Ian Macdonald there seemed something sinister about the mysterious caller who approached him as he was working late on a difficult job at about midnight on 14–15 November. The man – black-haired, about 26 years old, roughly 5ft 6in tall, wearing a grey and black checked coat and grey trousers – asked for a gallon of petrol to be put in a carrying can.

'He was not a local man,' the garage owner told the court. 'He sounded more like an Englishman than a Lewis man. He walked off in a westerly direction towards Brue Road junction [also the direction to Mary Mackenzie's house] and I saw him again at about 1am or 1.30am with a Ford van. It had windows in the sides.' The man then asked him for four gallons of petrol, at which point Mr Macdonald said he noticed some airline travel bags in the back of the van – and that the last two letters on the van's registration plate were SB. He paid with paper money and was given change – although, in answer to Mr Daiches, the garage man said the police had made no examination of the notes in his cash register after he had mentioned the matter to them on the following Saturday, when he heard of possible foul play in connection with Miss Mackenzie's death. And on that same day, he had seen the van again, being driven in the Stornoway direction, although he had not noticed the driver. He had also mentioned this to the police, he told the court, but had heard nothing further from them.

Later, Ian Macdonald talked disparagingly of the trial: 'All I remember was parading up and down a corridor in Inverness as the last but one witness to be called'. He spoke sympathetically of George Macleod: 'He went to sea and managed to keep his head very well.'

But what of the dark stranger? Macdonald clearly kept his suspicions, saying later:

I remember that, when he first asked for petrol, he had difficulty scraping up the money to pay for it; in fact, I don't think he even managed to find enough for a gallon. Then, when he returned, he seemed to have plenty of paper money. I can't now remember exactly what kind of notes they were, but I thought it all very odd, especially as the man was a complete stranger to me. And after I caught that glimpse of his van on the Saturday, I never saw him again.

12

Bible John's Fatal Charm

> SURPRISING AS IT MAY SEEM, his fantasies, interests
> and practices do not always make religion unacceptable
> to him, and sometimes there is not only a declared inter-
> est in it but he may be a church attender. He can also be
> sanctimonious and sometimes quote scripture... He may
> describe opposing forces warring within him, referring to
> them as Good and Evil or God and the Devil.

So wrote Dr Robert Brittain in his paper 'The Sadistic
Murderer', prepared in response to a request from Strathclyde
police for his help on the 'Bible John' investigation. The
consultant forensic psychologist suggested that, while
some sadistic sexual offenders might have characteristics
that support the average preconception – brutish, of low
intelligence, aggressive, insensitive, rough, crude, vulgar –
'the majority appear to be much like other people'.

Just like Bible John?

Yes and no. This particular monster, believed to have
murdered three women in relatively quick succession in the
late '60s after nights out at Glasgow's Barrowland Ballroom,
now a pop concert hall, certainly appeared to be quite the
opposite of brutish – if we are to believe the description we
have of him, which has been called one of the most precise
in Scottish police history. But he was not, in the context of
his operating environment, quite 'like other people' either.
Paradoxically perhaps, the man thought to be Bible John

stood out in the raucous Glasgow dancehall crowd because of his very 'respectability'.

The sister of one of his presumed victims said simply: 'He was not the Barrowland type.' The Barrowland type was loud-mouthed, aggressive, fashionably long-haired, and probably much the worse for the drink he had consumed before launching himself into the dancehall's mass of gyrating bodies. 'John' was different because he didn't drink or smoke; his reddish-brown hair was unfashionably short and neatly trimmed; he was tall and rather delicately handsome, polite and well-spoken with a soft Glasgow accent; and although he was in his late twenties and did wear reasonably modern clothes such as Italian-style suits and high-sided boots, the impression he gave was of a well-brought-up professional or military type with considerable charm. Altogether, something of a ladies' man.

His interests apparently included golf and religion.

It remains ironic and deeply puzzling that such a clear description – which included details like a slight overlapping of one front tooth across another – should not have delivered the man into the hands of one of Britain's most hardened police forces which, with much less to go on, has tracked down many a major criminal working in much more covert circumstances than a dancehall packed with potential witnesses.

Part of the problem was, however, that many of these people should not have been there in the first place: they were fugitives from shaky marriages, or less than faithful boyfriends or girlfriends looking for a little 'something on the side'. So – even if they could conceivably help – they were reluctant to come forward for fear of having to go public and being found out by their usual partners.

At first, too, there was no reason to believe that a triple

murderer was at large. In a city with more than its share of violent crime, the occasional case of a late-night quarrel going fatally over the top was just one of those unfortunate things that would soon become no more than a vague memory. Nevertheless, the shock was real enough when, on a raw February morning in 1968, Maurice Goodman walked towards his car lock-up in a quiet lane in Langside and discovered to his horror the dead and naked body of...

Victim No. 1

The previous Thursday evening, vivacious 25-year-old nurse Patricia Docker had asked her parents, with whom she was living at Langside, if they would look after her four-year-old son – from a broken marriage – while she went out dancing to the Majestic Ballroom. They were happy to do so, for she was a hardworking lass who deserved a little relaxation. But they never saw her alive again.

Exhaustive police enquiries proved, after many wasted days of checking out false leads from that establishment, that she had not been there at all. She had been at the Barrowland Ballroom. And by this time, memories had dimmed – or were consciously made to dim – for Thursday was the most 'secret' night of the week for over-25 dancers who preferred not to reveal their presence there.

Although the police did offer to preserve the anonymity of any witness coming forward, they qualified this by saying that the offer would have to be withdrawn if any useful material evidence were forthcoming. Not surprisingly, the only response they got was complete silence.

Faced with the dismal prospect of failure, the police could only go over the known ground again and surmise that Pat

Docker had been the victim of someone who had taken her home from the dancing, for her body had been found very near to her parents' house. From that point, there were certain things they knew: she had been strangled, suggesting a certain premeditation; she had been menstruating and there was no clear evidence of sexual assault; there was no sign of her clothes, as if her killer had taken some trouble to remove and conceal them; and a neighbour had reported hearing a female cry of 'Leave me alone!' the night before the body was found.

The nurse's estranged husband, an RAF man based at Digby, Lincolnshire, was checked out. Although he had been on leave in Scotland at the time, his parents said he had been at their home in faraway East Lothian on the night of the murder, and in St Andrews the following day. He was traced there to be informed of his wife's death and agreed to go to Glasgow to confirm identification of her, but he could offer no clue to her recent activities since he had not seen her for four months.

Although her handbag was eventually found in the nearby River Cart, it did not yield any clues. The only item police found, which was to prove significant in time, was a sanitary towel that had been lying near the woman's frozen body, which was curled up in a garage doorway. It suggested that the murder might have been the angry act of a man denied the ultimate sexual favour.

Frustrated as they were by the fruitlessness of their investigations, the police were wary of such facile speculation, but the clue took on a new meaning when, 18 months later, a group of children playing in a derelict Bridgeton tenement, reported finding the body of what was to be considered...

Victim No. 2

Jemima McDonald was a single mother of three children who liked to go dancing to keep her spirits up. And she didn't have far to go, for the rough-edged glamour and glitter of the Barrowland Ballroom was only about half a mile from her home, one of the few habitable tenements then remaining in the otherwise derelict area near Bridgeton Cross. But when the 32-year-old set off for the dancehall on the evening of Saturday 16 August 1969, wearing a short black skirt, white frilly blouse and high-heeled sling-back shoes, it was to be her last visit. She had left her children (aged 12, 9 and 7) in the care of her sister and neighbour, Margaret, who was not particularly concerned about her non-appearance the next day.

Not immediately, at least. Not until the 'body-in-the-house' reports of the neighbours' playing children, which had been initially shrugged off as a down-and-out sleeping rough, began to get too persistent and colourful. With mounting anxiety, Margaret waited another day for her sister to appear, then went to investigate the children's story. She was appalled to find Jemima's body lying in the bed recess of a tenement flat only a block away. Jemima was partly clothed and had been strangled with a stocking.

This time, the police's dancehall enquiries were to prove a little more illuminating, thanks to their promise that the 'domestic problems' of potential witnesses would be respected. So it came to light that Jemima had been seen leaving the ballroom in the company of an unknown man, and both had been seen walking through the late-night city streets. Within a week a sufficient number of sightings and descriptions of the man had been reported for the police to complete a fairly precise picture of him. It is interesting to note at this point the features that were soon to crop up again. He was described as slim, between 25 and 35 years old, at least 6ft tall, with short, reddish-fair hair, wearing a good suit and a white shirt.

Two of the witnesses who helped compile this picture, a boy and a girl, were asked to pin it down even more literally with the help of an American photofit system. But when they seemed less than confident about this, an artist was called in – Lennox Paterson, of Glasgow School of Art – who talked to them separately and frequently at some length. From these chats ('to the girl, the wanted man was almost like a film star and definitely a ladies' man') Paterson eventually managed to 'see' the man, to create an impressionistic but firm portrait of him; and for the first time in Scotland, the Crown Office sanctioned the publication of a picture of the suspect in a major crime.

The police were elated. The picture, published in newspapers throughout the country and shown repeatedly on television, was just the tool they needed in their hunt for the killer, and hopes for its success were high. But to their surprise, it made no difference at all and, slowly, the leads dried up again. Not even the offer of £100 reward, scraped together by Jemima's family, could tease out new clues, and those optimistic hopes turned into a sour disappointment which was not relieved by the dancehall's management calling time on the police presence there. Enough was enough, they said; with the best will in the world, they could help no further; and business, already suffering because of the two murders, stood little chance of recovering while the police were about.

Aware that they might need the management's cooperation again in the future, the police decided to preserve goodwill and pull out. It was a decision they were to regret bitterly. For no sooner had they done so than it happened again. Within a matter of days, and within several hundred yards of the safety of her home, the body was found of...

Victim No. 3

It was only ten weeks after the McDonald murder that attractive 29-year-old Helen Puttock announced to her surprisingly tolerant husband, George – home on leave from a British Army base in Germany – that she was going to the Barrowland for a night out with her sister, Jean. George raised no objection to babysitting their two children: as he missed them so much while away, he was happy to play the father role whenever he could.

Like Jemima McDonald, Helen was wearing a short black dress as she prepared to leave her temporary home at her mother's in Earl Street, Scotstoun, at about 8.30pm. George showed concern for her safe return, handing over some money for a taxi home as she and her sister departed, but he was never to see his wife alive again.

At seven the next morning – Friday 31 October 1969 – roadman Archie MacIntyre was out walking his black labrador when it suddenly made off excitedly towards what looked like a bundle of rags lying in a back court only a couple of blocks from Helen's home. Responding to the dog's whining, Archie went over to investigate 'and got the shock of my life: it was a woman's body and it was a funny colour.'

He rushed to a phone box and dialled 999. And when the police and ambulance services arrived, they confirmed that she was dead. She had been raped and strangled with one of her own stockings; one of her legs was thus bare, there was bruising to her face, and she too had been menstruating:

her sanitary towel was found tucked neatly under her arm. But nobody knew who she was... until, reacting to the flurry of police activity just down the street from where he was living, George Puttock emerged to tell the officers that he was worried about his wife's non-appearance. They showed him the body and his worst fears were confirmed.

Now the manhunt took on an unprecedented intensity. A maniac was clearly at large and had to be stopped before he struck yet again. And the chances of stopping him looked better than ever before – thanks largely to the remarkable recall of Helen's sister Jean Williams who had chatted to 'John' not only at the dancehall but also in a taxi shared with him and Helen part of the way home, and she thus proved to be a superb witness. She was highly valued as such by one of the key senior officers in the hunt, Detective Superintendent Joe Beattie, who personally interviewed her frequently and gleaned detail after detail with great follow-up potential.

Her meticulous description of the man who danced with her sister matched that of Jemima McDonald's last escort. She mentioned how his polite manner had evaporated as he exploded into anger at the management when the dancehall cigarette machine wouldn't work for Helen and how, on the shared taxi ride across the city, he revealed that despite being a non-smoker, he had had cigarettes all the time – produced a packet of Embassy, grudgingly shared them round, then pocketed them without taking one himself. He had made enthusiastic references to golf, telling a story about how his cousin had recently scored a hole in one. He had expressed disdainful attitude to the dancehall, describing it as a 'den of iniquity' frequented by 'adulterous women'. And there was his self-righteous statement, when asked what he did at New Year, that he preferred praying to drinking; his indirect quotation from the Bible, about Moses and a woman who had been stoned, was recognisable from the Old Testament.

In addition to all this, Jeannie was invaluable in enhancing the artist's impression of the man who was dubbed 'Bible John' thanks to the popular touch of a Glasgow newspaper editor. Indeed, her own picture of the man was so comprehensive that Superintendent Beattie said he now knew the suspect so well he would recognise him instantly if they passed on the street. It was a meeting that, alas, was never to happen. But not for want of trying.

Every conceivable angle was taken in the massive exercise to hunt down Bible John. No fewer than 100 detectives, now openly linking all three murders, were assigned to the case and every police force in the country was asked to cooperate. All the dentists in Glasgow were asked to check their chart records in an attempt to find the overlapping front tooth that might belong to a young man answering John's description; and all the city's tailors were asked to remember such a man ordering high-lapelled suits. Hairdressers' shops were checked out in the hope of finding someone who had done John's unfashionable trim; golf clubs were visited to try to track down his hole-in-one cousin; and because of his military bearing, British and NATO bases all over the world were asked to run through all their leave-pass records. A total of 50,000 statements were taken from nurses and newspapermen, dancers and dancehall staff, hoteliers and publicans, prison and Borstal officials, ministers and priests, doctors and mental hospital staff, bus drivers and taxi drivers – especially the one who drove the threesome home, though he could unfortunately remember very little about them.

At one point, the world-famous Dutch clairvoyant Gerard Croiset was called in to help. In response to feelers from the police, the Glasgow-based *Daily Record* brought him to Glasgow in the hope that he could add the Bible John case to his amazing list of psychic successes – which included finding, via the telephone, missing persons as far away from his Utrecht home as America and Japan. In this case the old Einstein-like figure immediately started to draw pictures from his mind of the area where he thought Bible John might be found and, with only the help of a city map, he indicated this to be in the southwest, around Govan. He then focused in on the place, describing old cars near a large defunct engine, schools, recreation grounds, and shops – one of which he pinpointed, sketching out descriptions of the shopkeepers and an elderly male customer who, he said, was somehow connected to the murderer.

Touring the area, a *Record* reporter found a location similar to this, near a main road, with old cars and a massive, rusting diesel engine. The police quickly responded, checking out the schools and shops and carrying out door-to-door enquiries. Once more, they drew a complete blank. Yet the lead was tantalisingly close to making sense. One witness interviewed earlier had reported seeing, on a late bus coming from the direction of Helen's home on the night of her murder, a bleeding, breathless and dishevelled young man who alighted near Gray Street, within walking distance of the terminal for the all-night ferry across the Clyde... to Govan.

Could he have been Bible John? If so, that was the last ever sighting of him. He remains doggedly elusive to this day, despite the assiduous efforts not only of the police and the media. Indeed, the media was so active in the hunt – there was even an BBC TV appeal to the culprit couched in biblical terms – that members of the public became in turn enthusiastic detectives. Young men who were unfortunate enough to look like the portrait of Bible John were constantly being challenged in the street. A printer called Norman MacDonald was so badgered by strangers that, once he had been eliminated from enquiries, he had to be issued with a special certificate from the chief constable to inform would-be apprehenders that he was definitely not Bible John.

But there were real suspects too. One result of a renewed police presence on the Barrowland dance floor – jokingly called the Police Formation Team and teased about eyeing up the men rather than the women – was the production of a rather elusive Bible John lookalike who, when finally apprehended and put into an identity parade, obviously did not look quite *enough* like the suspect. Jeannie Williams, who attended over 300 such parades, failed to identify anybody in this one and the man was promptly released.

The long, frustrating months turned into years with little or no progress to show for the thousands of arduous hours put into the investigation. But the longstanding impact of the case on the public imagination has been graphically illustrated again and again over the decades. In 1977, the *Record* pointed the finger of suspicion at a convicted rapist who had been to a dentist to have his two front teeth removed; he claimed this was because of a football injury. In 1983 a heating engineer suddenly went public with his private suspicions about his one-time best friend who, being a Barrowland regular and 'the double of the Bible John drawing', had moved to Holland; once he was traced, the episode ended in a farcical catalogue of denial, embarrassment and recrimination. At one point even Superintendent Beattie was 'shattered' to become convinced, as the investigation's lead detective, that the culprit was one of his own – a former policemen hiding out in the Highlands – according to a book by Paul Harrison.

One of the strangest aspects of the very strange Bible John story is the sudden appearance, and equally sudden ending, of his deadly works. If his urge to kill was so overwhelming that he had to yield to it three times, why did he suddenly stop? Or did he? There have since been similar murders in other parts of Scotland – and England, and even further afield – that remain unsolved. Did he simply move down south?

Pertinent to this theory is a certain Peter Tobin, who was convicted and jailed for life in 2007 for raping and murdering 23-year-old Angelika Kluk whose bludgeoned, stabbed, tied up and gagged body had been found the previous year under the floorboards of St Patrick's Roman Catholic Church in Glasgow's Anderston district where he had been working as a handyman.

Tobin (who once told a prison psychiatrist that he had killed 48 women) lived in the city during the sixties before moving south in 1969, the same year as the last two unsolved Barrowland murders. Criminologist Professor David Wilson, having studied the killer's record, once said he would stake his own reputation on Tobin being Bible John. Certainly, in the absence of any confessions from anyone, there are compelling pieces of evidence to make the link, not least the opinion of a Glasgow grandmother. In June 2010, after seeing a photograph of Tobin as a young man, Jean Puttock (now deceased) identified him to the press as the man with whom she and her sister Helen had shared that significant Barrowland encounter in the late 1960s – when she said the man had given the first name as John and his surname as Sempleton or Templeton. One alias used by Tobin was known to be John Semple.

There could be other explanations. Did the Barrowland serial killer simply die – naturally, accidentally, or even by his own hand driven by remorse? It is also possible that Bible John could have 'grown out' of his psychopathic tendencies and may have latterly chosen to lead a normal life, no longer driven by the compulsion to kill. To quote a leading psychiatrist: 'He will still be fully aware of what he has done in the past and will be carrying with him the terrible guilt and shame of it. But his conscience will not be strong enough to make him confess, although he will no longer have the urge to kill again.'

There is, of course, another theory which would demand a radical rethink of many assumptions. The three murders could have been the work of two, or even three, different people. And, of course, it is not unknown for follow-up crimes in a series to be committed by a copycat to throw all the blame on to the first culprit. Could the two later murders have been the work of two copycat killers?

There are so many possibilities, but the consensus of experienced opinion still tends to come down on the one-killer theory. And what is certain is that, despite all the high-quality description and evidence that police have had to hand, the killer of each of these women was clever enough to elude one of the biggest dragnets ever cast in any manhunt anywhere. And there is now very little hope of finding him unless something – something he reads in the Bible perhaps? – prompts him to come forward and come clean. But until that happens, his conscience will not be strong enough to make him confess.

13

The Unknown Bairn

THOUGH IT WAS a spring afternoon, the cold rain was spitting into their faces and the dark sky cast a miserable gloom over what was to have been a happy little outing for the father and his 5-year-old son. They were walking slowly along the shingle beach, kicking a few pebbles before them, wondering what to do next, when the father saw it first. A multicoloured floating object being washed back and forth perhaps 2 or 3 metres out in the grey waves lapping on to the southern bank of the Tay estuary. 'I thought it was a plastic doll.' As he was wearing wellington boots, he scrunched over the seaweed at the water's edge, waded in, grasped the object, and turned it over.

For Ian Robertson, a postman in the Fife town of Tayport, the afternoon of Sunday 23 May 1971 started off as a disappointment and turned into a black memory that he would never leave him.

At the pretty boating pond on the town's east end common, near the fast-flowing river, the weather had been playing havoc with a much anticipated event, the first model-boat race there since the beginning of the Second World War. It would have been just the thing to amuse his little boy, Neil, but when they realised it was going to be a literal washout, they turned away and headed across the shore track for a teeth-gritting walk along the nearby beach.

Less than a hundred yards from the pond, near a large jagged chunk of rock sticking up through the pebbles like a sore thumb, the discovery of the floating thing stopped them in their tracks. Puzzled, Neil waited as he watched the bundle being turned over; then, his father suddenly shouted to him to go home at once. He wanted to ask 'Why?' but the stridency in his dad's voice told him it was no questions asked order. He turned and ran home. Later, when he was older and could understand, his father answered his unasked question.

> When I turned the bundle over, it was a quite horrible sight – to see that it was a human body. A little boy about three years old. The nose and lips were almost gone and the knees were in a bad shape, all points where the body would have been in friction with the rocks or the riverbed.

With Neil safely out of range, Ian, trembling with shock and cold, brought the body on to the beach and ran back to the common, where the model-boatmen were packing up. 'I had to get one of them back to confirm what I had seen, it seemed so much like a bad dream.' And indeed, his volunteer saw the same ghastly sight and reacted with similar shocked disbelief. At once, they called in the police and soon the little body, wearing a patterned pyjama-type jersey over a blue shirt, was off to the pathologist in Cupar – who later officially reported that the boy had met his death by drowning, though there was a lingering suspicion, not least among the police, that he had met his death before he met the water.

But if the submission of his remains to the machinery of authority prompted hope that grieving parents would now materialise to round off the tragic matter with some dignity, to give the boy at least a loving burial, that hope was a vain one.

For, incredible as it might seem, to this day no one – not a parent or grandparent, not even a distant relative – has come forward to identify or claim him. And it could not be for lack of publicity (there was almost daily coverage of the story in the Scottish press at the time); or for lack of police effort, which stretched from the banks of the Tay to Interpol involvement in the coastal countries of mainland Europe. He must have come from somewhere; he must have been missed by someone. The alternative seems almost unthinkable: that he was unwanted, forcibly drowned, and allowed to slip away with the tide. But why? Such a fate is more commonly reserved for unwanted newborn babies. How many parents, however evil or distressed, could commit such a deed against a little one with whom they had lived for a few years? Or had he died with his parents, either accidentally or in a suicide pact? That might explain, to some degree, the lack of response. But where then did the adult bodies go? None was ever found that could be connected to the boy.

Interested people still visit the plot at the westside cemetery, seemingly in a belated effort to make up for the love that, somehow, the little boy lost along the way. But the grim fact that not all people are so compassionate and caring is also acknowledged here. For sometimes a plainclothes policeman may be watching those who come to lay down their floral tributes and say their silent prayers – on the assumption that a killer could be remorseful enough to visit his victim's resting place. And beneath his simple 3-ft stone, funded by the many charitable hearts, the little boy still seems alone, for there is a certain sad irony in the positioning of the grave – by itself, some distance away from the rows of community graves on the bank of the river directly facing the cityscape of Dundee; the very river that may have claimed his life.

The words on the plain-faced granite, engraved free of charge by local stone sculptor Robert Lawson, read:

Erected by the people of Scotland
In memory of THE UNKNOWN BAIRN
A wee boy
Aged between 2 and 4 years
Found on the beach at Tayport
23rd May 1971
'Suffer little children to come unto me'

The stone was not yet in place when the boy was put to rest five days after he was found. In contrast to that miserable afternoon, however, it was a fine sunny day that blossomed for the simple, if very well-attended, burial ceremony. In the absence of relatives, local undertaker John Beat carefully handed over the small, white-covered coffin he had made to the gravedigger 'who then descended some specially dug steps to place it gently in the grave'. The minister's accompanying words touched the hearts of the sizeable crowd that had gathered and there was many a silent tear, even from the hardened men of the police and the press, and certainly from those who had seen to it that at least the little lad was receiving a respectful farewell.

One such person was the then provost of the town, James Pow, who said a few poignant words to the press that still reflect the emotions of locals: 'My wife and I are heartbroken over this.' He later recalled his part in bringing the case to public attention:

When I heard about the finding of the body, I feared the arrangements for his burial were going to be pretty rough, so I organised a fundraising campaign with the help of the press, to give him a proper funeral and gravestone. It was amazing. The money just flooded in from all over Scotland and beyond and the townhouse staff couldn't do any

163

other work for a couple of weeks. We ended up with far too much, so the remainder went to the Scottish Society for the Prevention of Cruelty to Children.

And so, nearly five decades later, the mystery of the Unknown Bairn remains grimly unsolved and continues to haunt the people of Tayport who were involved in the affair. And even those who were not.

The story had clearly moved and mystified the whole country. Considering the coverage it received, it was impossible to imagine that the case had not also caused puzzlement south of the border and beyond. Wherever they were, the questions everybody asked were: did the boy fall in the water or was he put in? If he was put in, why? And if he fell in, why did the parents not come forward? And even if the parents had drowned too, where was the rest of his family?

But the police and the press, the two forces that could extract that truth if anyone could, were repeatedly frustrated at the time, and their efforts then were so tireless and thorough – the police pushing hard on many investigative fronts, the press diligently reporting progress and inviting feedback – that it now seems hopelessly optimistic to expect some lucky breakthrough in the future. There was perhaps a little justification for optimism in the early period of the investigation but, as the following diary of police daily reports shows, this slowly but surely soured into chronic frustration:

23 May Body found, police alerted. The only clue they find is the maker's label on one of his items of clothing: Achilles, size 3. They estimate the child found on the foreshore at high water mark beside the Tayport sawmill is aged 'about 2 to 3' and is almost 3ft tall.

24 May   Post-mortem asserts that death was due to drowning and that he had been in the water for 2 to 6 weeks.

25 May   Growing puzzlement over lack of family response to press reports. Detective Superintendent James Morgan, of Fife Constabulary, says: 'We agree there are suspicious circumstances. No child has been reported missing to our knowledge.' Appeals to police forces along the east coast and banks of the Tay, other UK forces, and the Missing Persons Bureau in London, all prove negative.

26 May   Inquiries extended to continental countries, British and foreign ships checked; so far in vain. The label clue has revealed that the shirt was made by the Leeds firm John Barren & Co, which distributed all over the UK and discontinued the line some 5 years before. Suggests boy came from less than wealthy family that clothed its children with hand-me-downs or second-hand items. Also suggests that he was British.

27 May   First possible breakthrough. Police say it has been established that a pair of child's Rainger wellingtons were found near the spot of boy's discovery 13 days before. Inside one leg, the name K. Gerrard had been written with felt-tip pen; the boots contained a pair of fawn ankle socks, and a clean white handkerchief was lying nearby. 'It is thought these may have been left by a child prior to paddling in the water.'

28 May   Burial ceremony. 'Provost Appeals for Gravestone for Unknown Child' is the headline in the *Dundee Courier.* 'I hope this appeal is not long under way before relatives of the poor wee bairn turn up to claim him,' comments Mr Pow. 'Often families split

up but usually there is a grandmother or somebody.'
Frustration is clearly mounting.

29 May   Money starts to pour in, but no progress so far on the
'wellington' lead.

31 May   Another promising tip-off. A couple of travelling
people have been overheard talking on a bus, from
Leven to Dunfermline, about a lost boy. 'I lost my
wee boy that day and he was only two,' the woman
is reported to have told her companion, a man with
long dark hair. She is described as aged 40 to 50,
short, with ruddy complexion.

1 June   Massive response to the provost's gravestone appeal.
Letters, poems, donations pour in to the town clerk's
office, including gifts of 75p from a group of five
Dundee children and 25p from 'Sharon, who cares'.
Local girl footballers donate all the takings from
their match.

2 June   The travelling folk lead crumbles. Police have
tracked down the couple to find that the woman was
talking about the day her son was taken into care.
But they say 'intensive inquiries' are still going on
among travelling communities.

5 June   Chief Superintendent White, head of Fife CID,
expresses 'amazement' at the lack of response from
the boy's family and says the 'wellington' clue has
been eliminated. He stresses that the victim was not
necessarily a 'travelling' boy. 9 June: A general alert
goes out to trace a 'tinker' woman who was selling
lavender in the area 'about three weeks ago'. Leads
are obviously becoming thinner and weaker.

10 June   As local, national and international police inquiries
yield nothing, what is perhaps the final hope has

to be abandoned. Suggestions that there might have been a connection with a body washed up at Kingsbarns two nights before, on the other side of the Fife peninsula, are discounted after it is revealed that the body – of an elderly woman with no teeth and wearing only the remains of a woollen vest and a corset – had been in the water for several months. 'It is thus considered unlikely,' said Detective Superintendent Morgan, 'that there is any link with the child found at Tayport.'

With a depressing certainty, the leads dried up and left the police scratching around for clues. Though they kept the case file open, there was nowhere left for them to turn. It seemed, and seems still, quite unbelievable that a little boy who once had a name, a family, a home, a language and a culture could, in death, no longer have anything to which he might be connected.

For the many people who cared, all that remained to assuage the frustration of not understanding was simple speculation. Yet most of their theories crumble under close examination.

A coastguard at Fife Ness, for example, suggested that the boy might have been washed all the way over from a continental country. 'I certainly wouldn't rule that out,' he said. 'Given the right wind and tide conditions, the body could have come right across the North Sea.'

But the British label on his clothes clearly suggested that he was, if not Scottish, English. And indeed, the coastguard had to concede that the 'more probable' explanation was that the body had been washed downriver. 'There are about three strong tidal streams around the Tay estuary,' he said, 'and they make such a complicated network that an object's movements would be almost impossible to trace back through them. It's a vicious river with very strong currents.'

Another popular theory – actually put forward in the early days of the investigation by Detective Superintendent Morgan himself – was that the boy had been on board a ship at sea with his family; there had been an incident and all had drowned. But there were no subsequent reports of sunk or abandoned vessels and no other bodies recovered.

After his retirement, free to speak more openly, he flatly rejected 'ship' and 'foreign' theories and found himself, after all those years, resorting to his still strong policeman's instinct:

> I can't really say why, but I always felt, ever more strongly latterly, that the boy was reasonably local and the child of poor parents who were perhaps too short of money to give him decent burial after accidental drowning and/or too embarrassed to come forward and try to do so while all the publicity was going on.

Why a 'poor' family?

> Well, all we really had to go on were his clothes and, while exposure to the water had certainly added to their wear and tear quite considerably, they were not of good quality in the first place and were also probably hand-me-downs... I felt he was a child of the travelling folk and had come down river from, say, Perthshire. They are, let's face it, a little lax about the bureaucracy that the rest of us have grudgingly learned to live with; they don't follow the rules, and it's not unknown for them to leave a death unregistered. But they are good people with their children, very fond and loving with them, and would probably be

very sad about not being able to give a youngster like this
a proper funeral.

As recently as 2018 his conviction was echoed by Bob
Beveridge, who had been a detective on the case. He told the
local press he was 'quite sure' he knew the identity of the child
but, inexplicably, felt it would be 'a shame' to reveal it. He
mentioned two travelling people who had been briefly held
on suspicion of being the parents, but who had been released
'because the evidence fell short'. He regretted that DNA tests
were not available at the time and that any such exercise would
now be too late, 'as the parents will be long gone'.

Whoever the parents were, it would be comforting to
imagine that they regretted the boy's passing in their own
way. Perhaps they sang their songs for him and prayed for him
around a camp-fire. For some people of nature, unable and
perhaps even unwilling to fund a 'proper' funeral, such an exit
might even be desirable; the most natural burial of all.

In any event, the Unknown Bairn must still be known to
someone, affectionately remembered, let's hope, by those who
nurtured him, played with him and loved him. In recent years,
he has been rather less alone, for Ian Robertson, the man who
found the little boy's body in the Tay, decided that he wished to
be buried as near as possible in the graveyard beside him. And
on his demise, so it came to pass.

14

Pilot Error... Perhaps

TO WALK OR drive around the magnificence of Mull, looking up in awe as you weave through haughty sheep contemptuous of your approach, is to realise just how small you are. Empty and looming, the island emphatically reminds you that it still belongs to God; that the tracks Man has made here for his little machines are but pathetic and barely tolerated scratches on its face. One of these scratches was put there in 1965, on the east shore of the Sound of Mull, ten miles south of Tobermory, by men of the Royal Engineers. It is a half-mile-long grassy landing strip attached to the wooden Norwegian-log Glenforsa Hotel and much used by its more prosperous guests with access to private aircraft.

One such guest, staying for a few days around Christmas 1975, was property manager Peter Gibbs. By all accounts, this former Spitfire pilot was an exceptional man – darkly handsome, much younger looking than his 54 years, separated from his wife, and still something of a flying adventurer. 'In flying he took things to the limit,' his son Michael said of him. 'He enjoyed doing exciting things; not exactly dicing with death but dicing on the edge of life.' And not only did he have a distinguished flying career behind him, he could also boast high flying achievement in the world of music, having been leader of the BBC Scottish Symphony Orchestra.

Although latterly based in Highbury, London, that harmonious experience had made him fond of Scotland, and particularly of Mull, which he knew well after many previous visits. Indeed, so enthusiastic was he about the island that he was contemplating the purchase of a hotel there, a subject that must have figured large in his conversations with his attractive 33-year-old friend, Dr Felicity Grainger, who accompanied him on the Christmas visit. They had arrived by car – Gibbs' elderly Jaguar – but there was no way such a man could ensconce himself in a hotel so temptingly near to an active landing strip without feeling an overpowering desire to fly. So when he heard that a single-engined Cessna 150 was available for hire across the water at Oban's North Connel airport, he soon had the machine back at Glenforsa with his hands on its controls.

He hired the plane from Ian Hamilton, a former Scottish sheriff with a colourful past who, as a student, had been involved in the controversial removal of the Stone of Scone from Westminster Abbey on Christmas Day 1955. He was not to know that his arrangement with Gibbs would involve him in big headlines again, exactly 20 years later. Nor did he know, as he handed over the plane he had bought for £3,000 the previous September (to service a market-garden business) that a month after that Peter Gibbs' flying licence had lapsed. When Gibbs explained that he had come on holiday without his licence because he had not expected to fly, Hamilton gave him the benefit of the doubt – also because his own telephonic inquiries, and the obvious expertise demonstrated by Gibbs in pre-flight checks, convinced him that here was an accomplished pilot.

It is probably fair to say that Gibbs' expertise then was as impressive as it had ever been; but his licence had not been renewed for other reasons. He was not as young as he looked, and, on applying for his renewal after a medical examination the previous May, he had been told to undergo a general flying test (which he had not yet done) and it was written into his record that he should wear spectacles to correct near/distance vision when flying. In he light of this problem, however slight he might have perceived it to be, the strange decision he took at around 9pm on Christmas Eve seemed all the more incomprehensible.

It was a fatal decision that was to create not one disturbing mystery but three, the one materialising on the heels of the other as each was solved. And to this day, the third has never been adequately explained: Less of a mystery, more a puzzle, was why in the first place such an experienced pilot should choose to don his flying-gear at that time of night on Christmas Eve, a few hours before his 55th birthday, and walk out of the hotel with the stated intention of taking off into the darkness. His companion Felicity Grainger, later claimed that he had been anxious to test himself and the airstrip for night landing, being of the opinion that its night closure inhibited its usefulness as the only strip on the island. 'It was just something that he wanted to know,' she said. 'It was not a sudden impulse.'

Yet it did not take any kind of a pilot to realise that an attempt even by someone with perfect eyesight to try to land on an unlit strip like this would be fraught with danger. Indeed, though he 'did not know much about airplanes', the then manager of the hotel, Tim Howitt, advised Gibbs that such a flight was not wise and tried to discourage him.

'He said he was not asking my permission,' Howitt recalled later, 'but letting me know his intentions as a courtesy and did not want any fuss.' Thus shrugging off the warning, Gibbs disappeared into the night with Grainger and soon the Cessna's Rolls Royce Continental engine burst into life. It attracted something of an audience: disbelieving guests gathered to watch its taxiing lights from the observation lounge that looked out across the Sound of Mull to the mainland, as Tim Howitt's brother David and his wife Pauline rushed out from their nearby chalet to look, astonished, through their binoculars.

From different vantages, both Tim and Pauline Howitt saw strange lights around the plane's wings before it took off. These were later assumed to have come from the two hand torches Grainger said she took with her to help guide Gibbs in. But the lights were alleged – by both onlookers – to have been too far apart to come from torches held by one person. And as Grainger later told an inquiry that Gibbs had not got out of the plane to assist her, this was another puzzling factor – was anyone else out there? 'I assumed,' said Tim Howitt, 'that there were two other people with torches.' In the absence of any further evidence, however, there was no development of this intriguing point. Yet it was a puzzle that could hardly compare in magnitude to...

Mystery No.1

Whatever happened to the plane and pilot? By the time the Cessna had revved up and taken off, David Howitt, who then supervised the airstrip, had walked down to within a few yards of the runway in time to gasp at its silhouetted shape roaring past his head at about a hundred feet – with its landing lights going off, on and off again. He could still see it as it climbed to about 800 feet out across the Sound in the direction of the mainland. When it turned on to an easterly heading, both he and the other observers assumed it was executing a normal circuit which involved turning back across the Sound and slipping briefly out of sight behind some high coastal pine trees, before descending to approach the runway from the east. 'This usually means an aircraft will reappear from behind the trees within about 15 seconds,' said David [who died in 2017]. 'But this plane did not reappear and, after a while, assuming Gibbs had another flight plan in mind, my wife and I made our way back to our chalet. That was when, turning back briefly, I saw the light on the water of the Sound.'

The light? 'Both my wife and I assumed it was a flare, which lasted perhaps 20 seconds before fading and disappearing. I then thought it possible that the plane might have undershot the runway and crashed into the Sound.' But he was less than convinced and preferred to believe that the light had come from a passing trawler... that the plane's pilot, wisely deciding that a night landing here looked too hazardous, had climbed well above the surrounding 3,000ft mountains and contacted Glasgow or Prestwick for a safer course to either of these airports with night landing facilities. And as such route-request communications could be intercepted by radio, Howitt hurried into his chalet, picked up his special set which could be tuned into aircraft transmissions, and scanned from 108 to 136 Mhz, hoping to pick up a distress call from the Cessna. But in vain. With a growing sense of unease, he then drove half a mile along the shore road, as near as possible to the point where he had seen the 'flare' on the water, and scanned the whole area with his car's headlights. Also without success. His unease began to border on alarm as, just before 10pm, sleet started to fall and he realised Gibbs then had no chance of returning to Glenforsa that night.

On his own return to the hotel, he found a shivering Felicity Grainger being comforted by guests. Paradoxically, while their anxiety was increasing – soon the plane would have no fuel left and the weather was rapidly deteriorating – she would hear nothing pessimistic. She seemed sure that Gibbs ('not a man to take risks') knew what he was doing and, explaining that she did not wish to spoil everyone's Christmas Eve by being unduly alarmist, asked that no telephone check-calls or alerting calls to the police be made until 10.30, by which time the plane could have landed somewhere else.

But the calls made immediately after that time established that it had not. Within half an hour, the first two-man volunteer search party was moving out of the Glenforsa Hotel, soon to become the frenetically busy HQ of a major search-and-rescue operation. But although this grew over the next two weeks into probably the biggest such hunt ever mobilised in Scotland, with police and mountain rescue teams and RAF planes covering a 150-mile radius, it proved frustratingly fruitless. Not the tiniest clue to the whereabouts of the plane and/or its pilot was uncovered.

It was as if they had vanished into thin air. And in the absence of rational explanations, the Great Mull Air Mystery began to take on irrational, even supernatural ones. The press was full of romantic theorising, the island hummed with wide-eyed gossip and invention. A local driver on the mainland swore he had seen the plane crash into the Sound – several weeks before it actually disappeared. The hotel room in which Gibbs and Grainger had slept became a room with a presence to be avoided because two other people who had stayed there also died in aircraft accidents: Prince William of Gloucester and Glasgow flying instructor Lesley Butler. Even the Howitt brothers' mother succumbed. She insisted she had seen a young man answering Gibbs' description walking across the Glenforsa runway in full wartime RAF flying gear shortly after his disappearance.

But in reality, her son David had, unknowingly, come nearest to the truth. As one half of that first urgently arranged search party on Christmas Eve – the other was local police constable

175

Alec MacLennan – he had trekked, through increasingly hostile weather, up hundreds of feet of spongy, slipper hillside (over which the plane would have descended on its final approach about a mile south of the runway) in the reasonable hope that if the crash had happened here, the pilot might still be alive. The two men separated and searched intensely through the trees and driving sleet with powerful torches. They were looking for something obvious, like flames or a broken wing protruding from the undergrowth. But Howitt later realised that, if he had known he was looking only for a man, things might have turned out quite differently...

For nearly four months later, when both men returned to the area on a bright April morning – summoned to help officials identify a body found by shepherd Donald MacKinnon – he realised that he could not have been more than 100 yards away from that spot as he searched the hillside that fateful night. The body was lying backwards over the fallen trunk of a larch, 400 feet up the hill from the now serene water of the Sound of Mull, and exactly a mile from the near-end of Glenforsa runway.

'Yes,' said Howitt, as he gazed on the once-handsome features, now grotesquely disfigured by weather and crows, 'I am certain that is Peter Gibbs.' Dental records later confirmed this. And Gibbs' clothes, though now faded, were as Howitt remembered them – lightweight cord slacks, checked shirt, pale blue pullover, and flying-boots. But the stench of decay was something he would rather forget, and he was glad to turn back down the hill with the vaguely satisfying feeling that at least part of the mystery had been solved.

But he hadn't reached the road at the foot of the hill before more questions began to raise themselves. If Gibbs' body had been there for four months, on a spot regularly passed by a shepherd with his dogs, why had it not been found before now? The body's legs had been straddled around one of the larch's upgrowing branches, as if trapping it in a fall – why would Gibbs have been coming *down* the mountain? And, perhaps most pertinent of all, the question that was to remain tantalisingly unanswered for more than a decade...

Mystery No.2

Where then was the plane? If the position of Gibbs' body suggested that he had been coming downhill, the logical conclusion to reach was that he had crashed and abandoned the plane at a higher altitude, not far from where he was found. Indeed, Chief Inspector Malcolm MacMartin, in charge of the inquiry, said as much: 'The reasonable assumption now is that Mr Gibbs crashed the plane somewhere up the hill, had a miraculous escape from death or injury, walked down the hill, and succumbed to exposure.'

But as the machine was nowhere to be found on nearby land, it was assumed – briefly – that it must have plunged into one of two freshwater lochs within a few miles of the body's final position. This theory did not hold up, however, on two major counts – the virtual impossibility of a shocked Gibbs covering so much difficult terrain to get to where he was found, and the shallowness of the lochs: a quick survey revealed that there was no evidence in either of them of leaked oil, floating debris, or protruding parts.

So perhaps, realising he was in trouble, Gibbs had simply jumped out of the plane and allowed it to fly on by itself to crash into the Sound below? Felicity Grainger claimed this is what Gibbs had always said he would do in an emergency; but the absence of serious injury to his body (there was only a 3-inch cut on the left shin) established beyond reasonable doubt that this was not what had happened. And at the fatal accident inquiry held in Oban on 24 June 1976, the Board of Trade Accident Inspector William Cairns maintained that it would have been 'extremely difficult' for the pilot to open the plane's door in flight.

With these theories thus more or less dismissed, and the plane still missing, the only remaining possibility seemed to be that Gibbs had indeed undershot the runway over the Sound, come down in the water, and escaped from the Cessna as it sank. This also became a highly unlikely explanation, however, after forensic tests revealed a complete lack of salt-water traces on his clothes, wristwatch, and flying boots.

But it did not lose all credence, as an element of possibility was raised when David Howitt published a book entitled *The Great Mull Air Mystery* – which suggested that the plane might have come down at a point, just short of the airstrip, where the River Forsa floods into the Sound and puts down a wide layer of *fresh* water on its surface. For some time, this appeared to be a reasonable supposition in the absence of any others, but it was eventually dramatically invalidated: one of the few questions to be answered by the long awaited development that had always promised to solve everything, as implied by Procurator Fiscal Graeme Pagan's statement in his inquiry summing-up that 'some mystery will always remain unless the plane can be found'.

The first tantalising clue to suggest that the plane had indeed crashed into the Sound appeared nearly four months after that inquiry – when farmer Robert Duncan found an aircraft tyre and inner tube on the shore at Kentallen, several miles north of Glenforsa. After it was established that the tyre would in fact match the Cessna, and that its covering of marine growth showed that it had been under water for a considerable time, attention was refocused on the Sound.

A subsequent sea search with sonar equipment revealed nothing, however, and the mystery began to grow again, although the evidence that the plane had undershot the runway and sunk remained compelling. Indeed, the little red and white Cessna was not to be found until every fantastic theory about its fate had been expounded by expert and layman alike... until, in fact, almost ten years later. And when it materialised in September 1986, its position was so far from the river-entrance that no further credence could be given to the idea that Gibbs might have swum through a top layer of fresh water to the shore, thus accounting for the lack of salt traces in his clothing.

The plane's finder was professional diver George Foster who, searching for scallops which tend to congregate in shadowy areas, went down to check out what had appeared as a 'promising lump' registered by his echo-sounder. Discerning a dark shape 100 feet down, 500 yards from the shore (and a mile and a half from the runway), he swam straight for it 'and saw to my surprise that it was the body of a plane'. The wings had been parted from it and he saw one lying flat in the mud about 100 yards away. The engine had also separated from the fuselage and one propeller blade was bent back as if it had suffered some impact. 'I didn't fully appreciate the significance of my discovery at the time,' said Foster, 'until I mentioned it to some mates on my return home; they got pretty excited and said I shouldn't tell anyone else for a while.'

But despite not appreciating its importance, Foster was curious enough to examine the wreck and recalled how, on peering inside the cockpit, he felt 'oddly disappointed there wasn't a body there'. He also noticed that the windscreen was

179

'completely out' and tried to enter the cockpit through it – 'but I just couldn't get in that way with all my gear on'. Still keen to see inside, though, he turned to the doors and tried to open them...'a devil of a job'. When he finally succeeded, all he found inside the cockpit was a large, sinister lobster.

He also noted the absence of compass and radio – and the presence of a single frogman's flipper in the mud, not far from the wreck. So had he in fact been the first to find the plane? He could not be sure. But what Foster's find had clearly established were two vital facts: one, that the doors of the plane had been firmly shut on impact and sinking; and two, that – despite the lack of salt traces on his clothes – Gibbs must have therefore scrambled out of the cockpit through the smashed windscreen. And those being the circumstances, minds would now have to be focused on yet another perplexing question in this constantly intriguing case...

Mystery No.3

Why was the body on the hillside? Accepting this scenario, it is not hard to imagine the desperate plight of Peter Gibbs in the Cessna's last airborne moments. Realising that he was undershooting into the Sound, he would have employed all his flying experience to retrieve the situation and, failing, would have been shocked and charged with adrenalin – fighting to save himself as the machine crashed into the water. He would have struggled out through the broken windscreen as it parted company with the wings, thrust himself up and away, then swum for the shore as if his life depended on it. Which it did. And this for 25 minutes over a distance of some 500 yards, through bone-chilling water and driving sleet: appalling conditions that would have tested younger and stronger swimmers to the limit.

Yet, having survived to reach the shore, why would he then have crossed two nearby, parallel roads – roads that would have led him straight back to the hotel's warmth and comfort in a few minutes – and opted to struggle on up the hillside for another 400 feet? Even further perhaps, considering the 'downhill' position of his body when found. It seemed nothing less than incredible that a chill-shocked, soaking and exhausted middle-aged man who had just miraculously escaped death should, for any reason at all, eschew the prospect of warm salvation within walking distance and choose to climb away from it into the hostile terrain of an incline that can be about 45 degrees in some places. It is a climb that calls for considerable exertion in the best of conditions, and on that night it must have been a nightmare of slithery banks, muddy pitfalls, and spiky trees and bushes. Not to mention two newly erected barbed-wire fences.

Medical experts have suggested that Gibbs might have been affected by a euphoric disorientation that can be brought on by concussion and would not therefore have been aware of climbing the hillside. But, unlikely though it might seem, he could also have had more rational reasons for making himself scarce after the accident.

Island gossip had it that a surfeit of alcohol could have accounted for what looked like an impulsive decision to take off that fateful Christmas Eve. Toxicology tests on his body had revealed a ratio of about 100mg of alcohol per 100ml of blood (the legal limit is 80) but conclusions were complicated by the presence of organisms, suggesting that this level was 'likely' to have been produced after death. So while Gibbs was thus officially considered not to have been intoxicated, it is known that at least a little wine had been drunk in his room before his fateful flight. Aware perhaps that even a small amount of alcohol in his blood – detected immediately after such a traumatic accident – would complicate his already compromised legality in flying without a licence, he might have simply chosen to sit it out for a while, assessing his plight before returning to the hotel.

Another popular theory was that he might have actually planned to disappear, to parachute from the plane, and that the plan had been thwarted by the severity of conditions encountered on the ground. Not far above the point where his body was discovered, two walkers came across what they swore was a parachute harness tucked under a rock; but the police, maintaining that it was merely from a rucksack, put it into storage.

Such a scenario would certainly explain the lack of salt traces on his clothing. But there are other ideas on this. One is that the plane could have crashed into shallow water near the shore, with Gibbs clambering out over the dry fuselage, then drifted out to the position in which it was finally found. Another, which would explain the non-discovery of the body for such a long period, is that he was actually put on the hill some time after his death... although, in finding that death was due to exposure, the medical officer at the accident inquiry, Dr WDS McLay, said that the body's condition 'was entirely consistent with lying out there for a period of four months'.

There was even talk of drug smuggling. An intriguing aside to this idea was provided by a fiction story anonymously submitted for consideration to Fiona Langford, editor of *Am Muileach*, the island's local paper. She felt it was too close to the real, controversial run of events to publish, but in essence, it suggested that a small plane from Glenforsa had a mysterious assignment to drop flotation bags, with waterproof lights, for picking up by a local trawler. It came down too low, crashed into the water, and its rescued pilot later died on board the boat. His body was such an embarrassment to the trawler crew that they later placed it on a nearby hill.

In contrast, the latest man in charge of Glenforsa Hotel and landing strip – another experienced London-born pilot, Brendan Walsh – has no time for such farfetched ideas. His no-nonsense view?

It was just stupidity... to go out flying on such a night when his eyesight and plane were not up to the conditions. Should we be surprised that he struggled out and staggered up the hillside in a state of disorientation?

Such an uncomplicated version definitely has some appeal. But in the perverse way of this bewildering saga, you might expect that, while it could initially offer matter-of-fact illumination, the idea that 'it can't be as simple as that' would inevitably grow again... and create more mystery. Conclusion? It now seems hopelessly optimistic to expect that anyone will ever really know exactly what happened to Peter Gibbs, the flying adventurer, on his last great adventure.

15

Missing, Presumed...

THIS WAS NOT, as Chief Constable Donald Henderson explained at Inverness a couple of months after it came to light, a missing-person case in the simple and understood sense of the phrase. 'It is a most peculiar mystery,' he said, 'and despite all the hard work that has been done, all we know is something a little more detailed about the lady's movements on the last day and a lot more about her relationships and her difficulties and things that might have caused it. But as to what happened, and how it happened, we have not got a clue.'

What the senior Inverness officer was referring to in January 1977 was the bizarre disappearance on 12 November the previous year of attractive local housewife Mrs Renee MacRae, and her 3-year-old son Andrew. It is a case that has continued to baffle police to this day; and about which the top detective in the investigation, Superintendent Donald Macarthur, said a decade later: 'Never a day passes but I think of Mrs MacRae and particularly the wee boy.'

Today's officers are no less concerned. Inverness-based Detective Superintendent Jim Smith says: 'We continue to urge anyone who may have information that could assist the investigation to come forward.' And the searches for clues have never been given up.

With its piquant element of the missing pair's still-unresolved fate, the enigma has puzzled the people of Scotland probably more than any other comparable case in recent years. One measure of the continuing public fascination with this unfinished story is that, whenever the compilation of mysteries for this book has been mentioned to anyone, the inevitable response has been: 'Oh! It will include the Mrs MacRae mystery of course!'

So how did it all begin, this tragic and bewildering tale?

At about ten o'clock on the Friday night in which Mrs MacRae and her son were later presumed to have disappeared, Malcolm Vaughan, a bus driver from Boat of Garten, was passing a lay-by at Dalmagarry, where the A9 cuts through desolate and misty moorland about 12 miles south of Inverness, when he noticed flames rising from behind the obscuring embankment. He stopped, looked again, and without further hesitation, went forward to investigate. Braving the fierce inferno, he found at the centre of it a metallic blue BMW 1602 turning rapidly into a skeleton as it was eagerly consumed by the flames. After checking there was no-one inside it, he stopped a passing motorist and asked him to call the fire brigade. But by the time it got there, there was little or nothing of the BMW's bodywork and interior left to save. Because of this near-total destruction, detectives were never able to check the car for fingerprints, although it did yield one small, possibly vital, clue...

But one of the first puzzling aspects of the affair was: why did the police take so long to get their investigation under way? They had immediately traced the ownership of the locked car, but without establishing Mrs MacRae's intended whereabouts or seeking to contact her, they left it until the following Monday to probe seriously the circumstances of the blaze and the mysterious vanishing of the mother and son from the scene.

The delay might have been partly because the car was found to be unoccupied and partly because no-one had reported Mrs

MacRae missing over the weekend. Her estranged husband, Gordon, had no reason to believe that anything was amiss, as she had told him she would be spending the weekend with her sister in Kilmarnock. In fact, it seemed she had other plans for those days, and her husband – with whom she had remained on good terms, despite their break-up – only learned of them later from her closest female friend who, after seeing the wreckage of the car on the Sunday, waited with mounting fear for Mrs MacRae's return. It was when his wife failed to contact him or pick up their nine-year-old son Gordon from school on the Monday that Mr MacRae also became alarmed. Clearly, something had happened to her and, with this realisation, his wife's friend, Mrs Valerie Steventon, felt obliged to reveal not only the fact that Mrs MacRae had a married lover with whom she had planned to spend the weekend – but also his identity.

When Mr MacRae, a director of a building firm, learned to his dismay that 'the other man' who had been having an affair of four years' duration with his wife was his own company secretary, William MacDowell, the unmasked lover was promptly dismissed. At this difficult time, the latter's embarrassment was doubtless compounded by a required admission of his clandestine affair also to the police; but he told them he had been at home all weekend after the 'tentative arrangement' to spend the days with Mrs MacRae had fallen through.

Meanwhile, after setting up a range of floodlights around the lay-by at Dalmagarry, officers began an intensive search for any clue left after a weekend of heavy rain. The car was taken to headquarters for forensic examination and, as Mrs MacRae's friend had mentioned that it had been giving some trouble, a BMW technician was flown up from Glasgow in an attempt to establish whether or not the car had been deliberately set on fire. Although these tests were inconclusive, there was that one small clue in the boot...

The priority at this stage, however, was to find both Mrs MacRae and Andrew – later revealed to have been fathered by MacDowell – dead or alive; and a massive search was launched into the wild terrain and bitter winter weather around the north's biggest town. It involved the intense combing of hundreds of square miles by police, army, civilian volunteers, tracker dogs, sub-aqua teams, RAF aircraft and civilian helicopters. Even the floorboards of Mrs MacRae's own bungalow (where she had been seen by a workman at about four o'clock on the Friday afternoon) were pulled up, and the foundations exhaustively searched. And at one point, a mechanical digger, ironically borrowed from Mr MacRae's building business, delved – without success – into a quarry once used during realignment and reconstruction of the A9 around the lay-by area. This led to local speculation that the bodies of the mother and son had ended up encased in concrete from the building work... a rather fanciful notion perhaps, though it was 'not discounted' by the officers involved in the search.

Yet no concrete evidence, literal or metaphorical, was forthcoming from their wide-ranging efforts in the field. Dozens of disused, water-filled quarries and tips were examined, every possible lead checked out. They brought in a hypnotist to probe witnesses' minds more deeply, and even followed up a claim by a spiritualist that she could pinpoint the separate burial-places of the mother and child after receiving messages from Mrs MacRae with the aid of an ouija board. Several hundred people, including all the members of the staff at Mr MacRae's building firm in the town's Harbour Road industrial estate, were interviewed and produced, among other things, two reports that his wife had been seen travelling in her car with an unidentified, moustachioed man in Inverness the night before her disappearance; and another report which referred to a man seen standing by a parked car about 200 yards from the lay-by where, about two hours later, Mrs MacRae's car was seen in flames.

Although the latter man eventually came forward – a German-based serviceman who was interviewed for the police by military authorities – neither he nor any other interviewees yielded any leads, despite a £1,000 reward for information offered by Mr MacRae. With such a paucity of evidence and witnesses, the mystery became foggier by the day. And the only clue remained the one found in the car...

There were, however, plenty of theories, and Chief Constable Henderson himself put forward no fewer than five: that Mrs MacRae had deliberately absented herself from home for her own reasons; that she and the child had somehow had an accident; that she had taken her own (and the child's) life; that they had been murdered by someone who was known to her; or by someone unknown to her.

The fact was, he pointed out, that the 37-year-old mother had given two different people two different reasons for going away. The last positive sighting was at her husband's office at five that night, five hours before her car was found ablaze... 'and from that moment on, there was neither sight nor sound of the woman'.

That there had been no sight of her was unquestionably true; but the matter of sound had earlier been intriguingly challenged by her self-confessed lover, a father of two teenage children within his own marriage, who claimed that twice during Mrs MacRae's first missing weekend his telephone had rung with the secret signal arrangement he and she had employed for the four years of their affair; he added that the police had even been present during the second 'call' – and his wife Rosemary, standing by his side despite his revelations, later expressed surprise that they had claimed to be unaware of this.

The implication was that Mrs MacRae had simply run away with her son and was trying to get a message through to her lover that they were all right. Which remains, of course, a possible scenario. Although one would still wonder why her car had to go up in flames, it might be reasonable to ask: had Mrs MacRae finally decided to call it a day and put some time and distance between her and the obvious stresses of a clandestine relationship that looked unlikely ever to achieve the relative dignity of openness? This idea could be tentatively upheld by the fact that detectives who searched her ranch-style bungalow – where she had gone to live with her sons just a mile from Mr MacDowell's home – found that she had been in the process of packing household goods and children's toys into tea-chests as if planning to leave quite soon.

Yet the theory could also lend support to quite another scenario put forward by her friend, Mrs Steventon, to whom she had confided many details of her otherwise-secret, long-standing affair. Apparently, the missing woman had spoken of a forthcoming move to live permanently with her lover in Shetland; it was alleged that she even had the room measurements of the oil company house which she said was waiting for them. But the existence of such a plan was not acknowledged by Mr MacDowell who, a week after the disappearances, emphatically denied to the press that there had been any such job, house, or intention.

So could Mrs MacRae have taken her own life, and Andrew's, to put an end to what Chief Constable Henderson called 'her difficulties'? The elementary objection to that theory is the absence of bodies: it would be practically impossible to commit suicide and perfectly hide away one's own corpse, not to mention someone else's, at the same time. And a similar objection – why no bodies? – must also apply to the accident theory.

Was it, therefore, murder? Despite, or perhaps even because of, the absence of bodies, the late Chief Constable Henderson himself never concealed his personal conviction, that that was the case. And there was always that one clue from the car that served to strengthen his belief...

Although they could not establish whether or not the mother and son perished in the blazing car, or indeed ascertain the cause of the fire which had obliterated all fingerprints and other possible evidence inside it, forensic scientists made a discovery that suggested physical injury with some connection to it: in the boot there were minute traces of blood which were later found to be of the same group as that of Mrs MacRae and Andrew. It was quite possible, of course, that the blood represented evidence only of some minor scratch sustained in an innocent task – such as the fetching of tools or the removal of a spare wheel – but it was also possible that it represented something more sinister by far. Simply: had the bodies of Mrs MacRae and her son been at some point secreted in the car's boot? And the presence of the blood in the car was almost as interesting to detectives as the absence of other things: where were the clothes, holdall, handbag, and blue canvas pushchair that Mrs MacRae was known to have taken from her house? Could the buggy have been used to transport the bodies?

In any case, these facts strongly suggested to the police the involvement of at least one other person. Had Mrs MacRae been with someone in the 'blank' five-hour period between being seen at her husband's office and the time of the car-blaze?

If so... who? And had this person been her killer? Had she and the boy been murdered in the car or elsewhere and later driven, in the boot, to the lay-by for disposal? If so, where did their remains disappear to? Was the car later deliberately set alight to destroy all potential evidence? Or had the 'troublesome' vehicle burst into flames by itself, causing the mother and child to flee from it, only to be picked up by an ostensibly helpful passing driver who abducted them? If so, why would the escaping Mrs MacRae, with child in arms, have wasted vital time locking the car? To this day, the questions go on and on and the case remains, as Donald Henderson put it, 'a most peculiar mystery'.

The Renee MacRae file remains open, however, with efforts to resolve the matter stretching over the decades. In 2004 a thorough search of Dalmagarry quarry was mounted by police, but no human remains were found. Two years later a report naming a suspect was sent to prosecutors – who decided, after considering it, that it offered insufficient evidence to prompt action. As recently as 2016 a ground-penetrating radar exercise indicated 'an anomaly' in the road surface near the scene of the car fire, perhaps suggesting bodies that had been buried there during construction... but it was eventually concluded that that section of road was not being built at the relevant time. And the police still get letters and verbal approaches claiming to reveal fresh information and leads, while they monitor changes in the key lives involved.

William MacDowell spent several years working for a construction company in the Middle East after the case hit the headlines, and Gordon MacRae rebuilt his life, having divorced the missing Renee in 1980 and remarried the following year. But he found it hard to forget the traumatic events of 1976, and said at one point:

Though the bodies of Renee and Andrew have never been found, there is no doubt in my mind that they were murdered. I have views on what must have happened but I have no way of proving them. I just wish that some new development would finally close the curtain forever.

That sentiment was echoed by the then Chief Constable at Inverness, Hugh MacMillan, who seemed confident the mystery would be eventually solved. 'People keep coming forward with snippets of information and thoughts that they didn't consider of value at the time,' he said:

We take them all seriously, even those claiming to have seen things in trances. And you never know… one day, someone might just walk in and say: 'I did it'. We are assuming, of course, that it was a matter of murder, but we can't be certain until one or both of the bodies are found.

How would such a discovery establish that?

Well, we don't even know for sure that these people are dead and, if we were to know, it could mean that certain relevance could be given to evidence already in our hands. The type of death and enlightenment on how and where it occurred could also be very helpful to the ultimate resolution of the case.

There is always the outside possibility, of course, that Mrs MacRae and her son could be alive and well and living in some foreign land where they have built a new and less complicated existence for themselves. But the police sense instinctively that this is highly unlikely. At one time or another over the years, a missing mother's love will cause a telephone to ring, a message somehow to be understood, a presence to be felt. And since that fateful weekend, there has been nothing.

Only silence.

16

Who Fired the Gun?

HE WAS something of a bulldog to look at, with dense, well-combed hair and deep-set eyes over a wry smile and Churchillian chin. But with more of a terrier's spirit; for, once he set his teeth into a target, William McRae simply would not let go. Ebullient and forceful, he was a man at once both feared and loved, a clever lawyer and one of the Scottish Nationalist Party's most memorable characters. Even the closest of his many friends could be taken aback by his passion and chosen causes... by the often unlikely avenues down which he drove his intellectual brilliance and dynamism. And he could make his opponents even less comfortable. His devastating and much too articulate frankness made him no friend, for instance, of certain sections of the British establishment against which he railed for much of his richly textured bachelor life.

But on the night of Friday 5 April 1985 – or perhaps early the next morning – that 61-year-old life of many dimensions abruptly met the beginning of its mysterious end at a bleak and lonely place on the A87 Invergarry to Kyle of Lochalsh road: one of the few spots in rural Inverness-shire that is more sinister than picturesque; where the landscape is angular and rocky and casts lifeless shadows, with no trees and little green. The perilous, narrow road on which he had been driving to his holiday crofthouse near Loch Duich, Ross-shire, plunges steeply down on the left-hand side through dry brown heather and scree to the faraway shore of Loch Loyne. A road on which the most reckless of drivers would go slowly for fear of meeting another vehicle coming the other way. But one way or another, this evil road claimed William McRae after one of its slower bends, in what at first looked like an unfortunate accident…

By a strange coincidence, the inquiry into the Atomic Energy Authority's controversial plan for a new reprocessing plant at Dounreay was to open exactly one year later. And after his 'accident' some suspicious minds suggested that certain establishment hearts might not have been gladdened to learn that this most active of human-rights activists was planning to participate in it; for his headline-grabbing words at a previous, similar hearing in 1980 – at which he represented the SNP in its opposition to proposed test drilling for nuclear waste sites in Ayrshire's Mullwharchar Hills – would not be easily forgotten.

'Nuclear waste,' he said then among other stinging comments, 'should be stored where Guy Fawkes put his gunpowder.'

The media loved it. His opponents flinched. And there was no doubt that, given half a chance, he would deliver more such telling rhetorical blows at Dounreay. But empty rhetoric wasn't his style. There would have to be substance to it. Was he getting his terrier's teeth into such substance as he set off on that Good Friday evening from his small office in Buchanan Street, Glasgow, taking with him certain files to study over the Easter break? No-one knows for sure, but friends who saw him leave recalled that he was bubbling with enthusiasm as he called out excitedly:

'I've got them! I've got them!'

Those cryptic words were as puzzling then as they are now, for they were never to be elaborated upon by William McRae. The next morning, with three-quarters of his journey behind him, his damaged Volvo was found – about 70 yards off the road, down the rough incline facing the loch – by a passing Australian tourist who, thoroughly shaken, flagged down the first car that came along. As fate would have it, the driver was another SNP member, Dundee councillor David Coutts, on his way to Skye for a family holiday. When he looked inside the wrecked car, he was shocked to recognise Mr McRae in the driving seat, still precariously hanging on to life in a state of coma, with bloody head injuries.

An ambulance quickly summoned, he was rushed to hospital in Inverness and then transferred to Aberdeen, where he died early the following morning. The morning after that, his obituary in *The Scotsman* began with the following sentence, which suggested simple acceptance of death by car-crash injury:

Mr William McRae died yesterday in Aberdeen Royal Infirmary after a car accident in the Highlands.

Seven more paragraphs outlined his life story, including his many achievements and occasional disappointments – like his failure, three times, to be elected SNP Member of Parliament for Ross and Cromarty – and that might simply have been that. But two weeks later the bombshell burst...when it was officially revealed that his death had been caused by a .22 bullet wound to the head.

Despite his friends' protestations that McRae was the last person in the world who would contemplate such a thing, the initially accepted assumption by the authorities and the general public was that he must have inflicted the fatal injury upon himself, having decided to commit suicide in this dark and isolated spot where he knew there would be no witnesses; he was, after all, known to possess a .22 revolver. But, strange to tell, no information about the ownership of the twice-fired death weapon was released. Even stranger, the information that did become available later – particularly the fact that the gun was found by police in a stream some 20 yards away from what must have been the scene of the shooting – served only to create more and more mystery. Indeed, with the emergence of each new fact, doubt and suspicion grew ever deeper, making official explanations increasingly difficult to accept. Eventually, there seemed to be too many anomalies in the case for the media and public to settle for the simple suicide assumption. For instance…

Mr McRae had apparently been shot above the right ear, but there were no burns around the wound consistent with close-range self-infliction. Another disturbing observation was made by Councillor Coutts who recalled that, when he came upon the crash scene, he found it 'peculiar that Mr McRae's watch, cheque cards and other personal effects were some way away from the car… a lot of things had been ripped up'.

The car's back window had been smashed too; and its ignition and door keys had been found on the dying man's lap. Also puzzling was the absence of the victim's briefcase and/or files which he was known to have taken with him; they appeared to have vanished without trace. But most bewildering of all was the matter of the 'thrown-away' gun.

Whose hand had created these inconsistencies and disturbances?

It is hard to believe it was that of William McRae who, if he had indeed shot himself in the head, would hardly have been in a fit condition to lob his suicide weapon 20 yards from the car in which he sat fatally wounded. The hand of a simple ransacking vandal perhaps, who had come upon the tragic scene later and tried to profit from it? Or could it have been…

and speculation was growing fast... the sinister and expert hand of a long-range marksman who was also a cold-blooded killer?

There was, after all, no shortage of hostile reaction to McRae and many of his works; there were even, it was said, low-lying and resentful enemies with vengeful intent. Alongside the many other causes he championed, McRae had been a persistent campaigner in international circles for Scotland's own legal and constitutional rights. It was also said that he had connections with militant nationalist groups. Indeed, his personal and political history and geography were littered with controversy. He was a well-travelled man who at one moment would be flying to meet business commitments in the People's Republic of China, at another lecturing on maritime law at the University of Haifa, at yet another chatting sympathetically in Urdu with an Asian client in his small Glasgow office.

While much loved and respected by those in his corner, he was also undoubtedly perceived as an annoying, even dangerous, thorn in the flesh of more than a few others. So was someone, some agency, trying to remove the thorn once and for all? One suspicious sign was the mystery of a fire at his house the day before he died. Another was the very date of his fatal 'accident'. Was it merely a coincidence that 6 April was Scottish Independence Day – the anniversary of the 1320 Declaration of Independence at the Abbey of Arbroath? Or was it a deliberate signal being sent to the more zealous nationalists whose most fanatical faction, the Scottish National Liberation Army (SNLA), claimed to have come close to murdering the Prime Minister with a bomb attack on the 1983 Scottish Conservative conference in Perth?

The questions are easy to pose. The evidence and answers are considerably more difficult to come by. To the central question, for example – who, specifically, would want to silence William McRae and why? – there are too many possible answers with very little beyond the circumstantial to support them; a positive plethora of hypotheses that range from the simplistic through the plain foggy to the utterly fanciful. In rising degrees of complexity, starting with supposed justifications for taking his own life, they went something like this:

Rumours went round – and surely his friends didn't start them – that he was homosexual, which supposedly made him susceptible to emotional instability and perhaps even blackmail.

Having been convicted in the past for driving over the legal alcohol limit, he was fearful, some said, of more shame. It was hinted that being on the brink of another such prosecution had made him apprehensive and depressed enough to take his own life.

There were suggestions, allegedly based on his own statements, that McRae had been trying to help stamp out drug smuggling on the west coast of Scotland and had thus incurred the traffickers' displeasure, making himself an obvious target for a hitman.

Because the proposed new reprocessing plant at Dounreay was of such supreme importance to the area in terms of employment, could there have been some local party who believed that a powerfully persuasive voice against it – such as McRae's – would be best pre-emptively silenced by fair means or foul?

Some of the media suggested he was too close to the bellicose nationalist militants, which could mark him as an 'enemy of the state'. Indeed, a 1988 article in Carn, journal of the Celtic League, quoted the SNLA as claiming, in a clandestine newspaper, that McRae had been 'an active

199

sympathiser' who had assisted them financially as well as in planning attacks; the SNLA had also accused the British state of 'the murder of Willie McRae and of attempting a crude and ineffective cover-up'. And finally...

A correspondent to *The Scotsman* suggested that the lawyer could also have been regarded as an enemy of the state for more historical reasons. Alan Clayton, a one-time fellow member of the SNP's strategy committee which often met at McRae's Glasgow office, wrote that, while McRae was with the British Army in India between 1945 arid 1947, he maintained a clandestine contact with the Indian National Congress and that:

It was due to this 'early warning system' that an illegal and peripatetic liberation radio station operating around the New Delhi area was able to stay one step ahead of the British Army during the liberation struggle. Such activity, of course, rendered him liable to the firing squad. British security was unable to prove these activities, but neither did it forgive or forget...

After several other allegations of activity liable to upset the British establishment, Clayton concluded:

To my mind it is abundantly clear that William McRae was a well-established, dangerous and deadly enemy of a state which will go to apparently any lengths to sustain and protect itself.

These ideas were promptly countered by another letter writer, James MacRae – 'a close friend from 1940 onward, particularly during his university career' – who pointed out that William McRae had been an officer in the Royal Indian Navy (not the British Army) and that by 1947 was 'well into his law degree course, having resumed his studies on the same day as I, in October, 1946'. He went on:

I know that at the time his sympathies were more with Pakistan than India. In any case, why 'clandestine' contact with the Indian National Congress? When I left the Far East in September, 1946, the establishment of Indian independence was generally regarded as an imminent certainty. A well-established, dangerous and deadly enemy of the state? No, no, Mr Clayton, I cannot accept that.

He ended with a plea that his friend be allowed to rest in peace.

But considering the undying strength of the controversy, it seemed most unlikely that William McRae would be allowed such a posthumous luxury.

Although a good deal of that controversy (and the popular theorising outlined above) took place two or three years after the original incident, many nagging questions had already arisen within months of it and, to try to set them to rest, the pressure inevitably mounted for a fatal accident inquiry. At first, the chances of one being set up looked promising. Although the procurator fiscal at Inverness, Thomas Aitchison, had initially said there were no suspicious circumstances to merit such an inquiry, he conceded in mid-June of 1985 that 'that was before other matters were raised; now all sorts of factors are coming into this'. He also admitted that the Crown Office in Edinburgh had asked him to continue inquiries after he submitted his original report on the death. And the Solicitor General, Peter Fraser, agreed that if there were any real degree of public concern about the circumstances of the death, he would be 'prepared to consider' a fatal accident inquiry.

To the astonishment of the many interested parties, however, the Crown Office announced a little over two weeks later – roughly three months after McRae's death – that there was to be no inquiry. Its statement said that a full report on the death had been considered and Crown counsel were satisfied that there were no circumstances to warrant criminal proceedings or public inquiry.

The two men who had fought most vigorously for the probe-that-was-not-to-be were Bob McTaggart, Labour MP for McRae's constituency, and Councillor Coutts, who had first recognised his unfortunate colleague in the wreck of his car. In his campaign, McTaggart had declared: 'I just want to get to the bottom of this. If Willie McRae committed suicide it was a very strange way of doing it… it just doesn't gel with me…I would like some answers and I would like to see a public inquiry.' Both campaigners' subsequent reluctant acceptance of the negative official decision seemed strange at first; then it became clear that they were respecting the wishes of the dead man's family – his next of kin was his brother, Dr Fergus McRae – who, according to the Solicitor General, wished to see no further inquiries. And a letter from the Crown Agent dated 22 July stated flatly that 'no further information on the circumstances of this death will be made public'.

If some hoped that this would finally put speculation to rest, however, that hope was clearly too optimistic. The mystery refused to lie dead and buried with William McRae. Doubts persisted and the SNP, anxious to quieten some of its louder voices on the subject, set up its own investigation headed by the party's widely respected stateswoman, Winnie Ewing, not only a lawyer herself but also Euro MP for the Highlands and Islands.

In the course of her inquiries, Mrs Ewing contacted a close friend and political associate of McRae, Michael Strathern – despite, or perhaps because of, the fact that he had been expelled from the SNP for being a member of the proscribed direct action group *Siol nan Gaidheal* (Seed of the Gaels). 'Many of us had hoped,' she wrote to him, 'that Willie could lie undisturbed but it appears that...the Press will not let this happen.' She added a list of no fewer than 33 questions that she reckoned had not been satisfactorily resolved. Strathern's response welcomed her inquiry because those questions (covering time of death, state of the car and personal effects, the police and procurator fiscal's investigations, the gun and the bullet) were the very ones he and others had been trying to get the Crown authorities to answer. In the kind of colourful language that would have delighted his late friend, he added this observation:

> From the beginning of this strange tale I have had a powerful sense of the presence of Willie McRae standing at my shoulder and declaring in far-from-dulcet tones, 'For God's sake do something about it'.

Nor did Strathern mince his words to the press. He had, he said, tried hard to see the incident as suicide but all the facts spoke against that explanation, as did McRae's character.

> He had so much still to do. If it had been the day after Scotland had won independence, his work would have been done and I might have believed it. But all the facts speak against it being suicide. And the claim by the Solicitor General and the Crown Agent that there were no suspicious circumstances is too preposterous for serious

consideration and must give rise to suspicion in itself.

Ewing made her move. Almost two years after the incident happened, she applied for access, as a lawyer, to the procurator fiscal's official papers relevant to the case. The idea was that, in the anticipated negotiations, she would offer an undertaking of confidentiality if, on reading the material, she accepted that there were no suspicious circumstances. In other words, if she felt the evidence did indeed point to suicide, the SNP would no longer pursue the matter. But in the event there were to be no negotiations. She was promptly rebuffed – a blunt statement from the Crown Office said previous requests had been turned down and there was no reason to think a new request would be treated differently – and to the surprise of many who were following the case, the party then appeared to give up without a fight; all it could officially do was 'regret' that decision.

Though it certainly looked as if she had backed down reluctantly, Mrs Ewing would make no further comment on the case; but the surprised, bitter disappointment in some of the more-zealous nationalist circles was not confined to the same grudging resignation. They began to suggest openly that Mrs Ewing had learned something, somehow, in the course of her inquiry that had had the effect of cooling its intensity. The inevitable elaboration was to allege that – militancy being perceived by voters as a negative factor in a political party's electability – McRae had been disowned by the SNP hierarchy for the same reason that he had been murdered by the security forces: that he was too close to those prepared to resort to force for the nationalist cause.

Could there conceivably be anything in that? It seemed appropriate to ask the chairman of the party, Gordon Wilson. His response was:

There may have been some mystery about Willie's death, but there was no mystery about the end of our inquiry. There was simply a limit to what could be done. We would have liked access to the papers, of course, but there was no legal precedent for such a procedure and, having decided it was suicide and having made the no-inquiry decision, the authorities were then just immobilised by their own bureaucracy. Once decisions had been made, they couldn't be changed. But it's important to remember that, at the very beginning, before the relatives made their feeling clear – that they believed it was suicide – the authorities had not been unwilling to consider an inquiry. In fact, the Solicitor General even approached me at the time to ask if the party wanted one. I spoke to the relatives and they said they'd be very upset if there were one.

But, speaking hypothetically, would the party (or the family) have found a sympathy between McRae and the direct-action zealots unpalatable? 'Well, are there any such advocates of violence?' asked Wilson, adding:

The SNLA? Who are they? Do they even exist? Have you ever seen them, or any damage they've done? I certainly haven't. But if they did exist and if Willie had had connections with them, yes, the party would have found that slightly embarrassing; but no more than that. For latterly, he wasn't such an influential figure as he had been. He certainly could not be seen as representing the party's stance on anything. His influence had been greater in the 60s and 70s.

So was the party boss saying that he saw nothing sinister in his death at all? He explained:

I accept that there were a lot of questions that should have been answered publicly – though, after the passage of time, I doubt now whether they could be answered adequately – but my own feeling has always been that it was suicide. Willie had a lot of problems about which he could get depressed, not the least of them being his health.

In Wilson's opinion, could there have been anything to the security forces' allegation? There were, after all, reports that McRae had claimed jubilantly to friends, in the days before his death, that he had made a breakthrough in his work that would soon have the Special Branch closing in on him. Wilson surmised:

It's always possible, of course, that it was a sinister action by officers of the British State, and after the SAS killings on Gibraltar, I'm almost willing to believe anything. Almost... but I'd need to be convinced.

Be that as it may, with his party's retirement from the ring, others felt the obligation to keep the McRae flame alight in a less official but more passionate way, in keeping, perhaps, with the campaigning spirit of the man. To pay their respects and express their displeasure at what they perceived as the inaction of the authorities, friends and other interested parties got the protest show on the road again – literally. The A87 road, where the Volvo had originally come to grief. They began a tradition of regularly visiting the site of the incident – now marked with a cairn of rocks from various parts of Scotland – and speaking their minds into the biting wind.

When nearly a hundred of them first gathered in 1987 to erect the memorial cairn on an outcrop of rock high above

Loch Loyne and not so far above what had been the scene of the crime-that-never-was, it seemed that Councillor Coutts had found his voice again as he joined other calls for more information on the affair. He recalled that, for that very purpose, he had contacted the Solicitor General, the Lord Advocate, and the procurator fiscal at Inverness 'and the wall of silence that has been put up suggested to me that some department has something to hide'.

With the magnificent, malevolent view across the loch stretching out behind him, a piper played a lament and a eulogy was given by Michael Strathern as the Scottish flag was raised after fluttering at half-mast on the nearby flagstaff. He spoke of William McRae as a great Scottish patriot who, like Martin Luther King, Gandhi and others, had lived with the constant threat of an assassin's bullet. And later, with unequivocal boldness, he said what was on the mind of everyone who had made the pilgrimage to that sinister place:

> There was nothing suspicious about Willie's death – he was murdered, otherwise we wouldn't be here. I can think of two factions who would have wanted him dead.

But wait! As recently as 5 April 2015, on the 30th anniversary of the death, there appeared to be a breakthrough supporting the suicide case, when a *Scotland on Sunday* investigation offered an explanation of why the gun had been found so far away from the car:

> Previously unseen police reports show that his Volvo was removed from the crash scene before the gunshot wound was found... and when it was returned it was placed close to the original site but not in the precise spot.

Exactly one year after that, however, the *Sunday Herald* brought that into question again when it revealed that the weapon allegedly used had been neither fingerprinted nor subjected to forensic examination – and had disappeared with no administrative record as to why it was discarded, where it might have ended up, or when it vanished. 'So vital evidence to support the assertion that McRae committed suicide does not exist.'

Who, then, is right? It is not uncommon, of course, for those who hold strong political views to find their way through often imaginary mazes to the kind of conclusion that others would consider unlikely at best. But, perhaps paradoxically, such exotic plants grow best on the thinnest of informational grounds. And there is no doubt that in this case more official enlightenment would have led to less public suspicion, less fanciful hypothesising. Perhaps it is not too much to hope that the answers to at least some of the nagging, outstanding questions might yet be forthcoming. But until they are, it seems regrettable that the impartial observer of this perplexing mystery must make a simple choice between two highly unsatisfactory explanations for its existence: immobile bureaucracy or sinister conspiracy.

Ironically, perhaps the man best suited to blast open such a case would have been the sharp and colourful William McRae himself. A man who was unquestionably larger than life, and who is now – thanks in some measure to the system he challenged so energetically when he was alive – a good deal larger than death.

17

What in Heaven Was That?

WASN'T THE CELEBRATED presence of Paul McCartney enough for the beautiful Kintyre Peninsula to attract world attention, or at least more tourists? One of the lines in the ex-Beatle's famous musical tribute to the area, *Mull of Kintyre,* was 'Oh, mist coming in from the sea...' His band at the time was Wings... rather apt, you realise now, for not long after that big hit something more sinister seemed to be coming in from the sea – on wings – to that far southwest corner of Argyll.

Were the local folk just cultivating a revenue earning rumour about The Thing or could it possibly have been true? In truth, the more qualified gossipers would probably have been incomers with some inside knowledge letting the cat (if it did exist) out of the bag. In any event, mysteriously sourced tales about it persistently prompted breathless, if baffled, media accounts.

So what was the specific thing they were on about? Was it a bird, was it a plane? The consensus seemed to be that it was the latter, and a very strange plane at that. A Scottish newspaper reported in 1992, for instance, that a jet travelling at more than three times the speed of sound was being tested near Machrihanish air base. Who had seen it? 'Three or four farmers and two or three security guards and the occasional drunken builder all had their names in this article and we were in hysterics because it was simply make-believe,' said a sceptical RAF corporal interviewed for a feature by the same paper some years later, because he had been based there. 'Paul

McCartney hadn't brought in enough tourism so they needed something new.'

But the cloak-and-dagger stories kept coming and the question still had to be asked – if it existed, whose thing was it? Questions asked in the UK at the highest level went unanswered and its suspected guardians – America's defence chiefs – denied any knowledge of anything like that. But later that year another report, emanating from an American aircraft industry source, had doubled the phantom machine's speed while using the name it seemed to have acquired in the meantime... Aurora. Which turned out to be – probably – the name of a project rather than a specific machine, christened thus in US defence budget listings to fudge a secret 'black aircraft production' entry for a then-huge sum apparently bordering on half a billion dollars.

This report asserted that 'Aurora' was being flown from a base in the Nevada desert and on to Scotland to refuel before returning to the US at night... and that 'specially modified tanker aircraft are being used to top up its tanks with liquid methane fuel in mid-air'. It went on:

> The US Air Force is using the remote RAF airbase at Machrihanish as a staging point... The mystery aircraft has been dropping in at night before streaking back to America across the North Pole at more than six times the speed of sound... An F-111 fighter bomber is scrambling as the black-painted aircraft lands, flying in close formation to confuse prying civilian radars.

Such reports had been appearing on and off since the mid-1980s, often mentioning the Machrihanish air base; but if that facility was involved in the development of some astonishing new US war planes, why would that be?

It would be because the place was far more important than it looked.

Inaugurated during World War Two as RAF Machrihanish (after the village of that name), the base was a deal more interesting than your typical rural airstrip – boasting one of Europe's longest runways (nearly two miles) whose entire surface was regularly painted to match the surrounding undergrowth.

Located at such a strategic point on the eastern edge of the Atlantic – at the bottom western corner of the peninsula directly across the landmass from the main town of Campbeltown – it was used to guard the entrance to the Firth of Clyde where US nuclear submarines were based at Holy Loch and where Royal Navy Trident missile submarines are still based at the Faslane Naval Base. Throughout its operational existence (before ceasing military work in 1997) it hosted RAF squadrons and other NATO air forces as well as the United States Marine Corps; not to mention (it is said) a large, secret underground facility guarded by elite troops from the US Navy SEALs.

It was conceived to be used as an Emergency Airfield Over-flow (EAOF) able to cope with any aircraft landing with technical problems, including the Space Shuttle should it need to make landfall in Europe, the Russian *Bear*, and the P-3 Orions of the Royal Norwegian Air Force, who used the base in the context of NATO exercises.

(It is perhaps interesting to note here that the peninsula was once 'owned' by Norway – after its King Magnus launched a military campaign in 1093 to forcefully assert his authority over the isles. Scotland's King Malcolm proved accommodating, offering a written agreement that the Norwegian ruler would have sovereign authority over all the western lands that he could encircle by boat. The message's vague wording allowed Magnus to have his boat dragged across the narrow isthmus at Tarbert – while he rode within it – so that he thereby 'acquired' Kintyre, despite its not being actually an island.)

Such important international activities were inevitably going to make the Machrihanish base subject to rumour and bizarre speculation. It was widely believed that its super-long runway, facing east–west in such a remote part of Scotland, could enable aircraft to approach from the sea unobserved – ideal for covert or secret movements. Which appealed especially to UFO believers, one of whom observed:

> Machrihanish would be an ideal spot from which to operate aircraft technology that the Government wanted to keep secret... the perfect place for testing top-secret spaceplanes.

So was it such a thing that Chris Gibson saw from a North Sea drilling rig as early as 1989? And why should we care what this particular person saw? 'They' should care anyway, because, if they wished to hide a top-secret, highly developed, hypersonic superplane from anyone in or around Britain, his eyes would the last they would want to fly it over. For Chris – a Scot whose day job is as a rig engineer – describes himself as an aircraft recognition specialist and has written no fewer than ten books on related aviation projects.

As a one-time member of the British Royal Observer Corps, he was part of its aircraft recognition team for ten years and so was trained to identify 'any aircraft in service around the world'.

And yet, and yet...

He failed to recognise the one that flew over his head that

late August afternoon while he worked on the jack-up barge GSF *Galveston Key* in the North Sea. What he and another witness beheld to their fascination and astonishment was an unfamiliar isosceles triangle-shaped delta aircraft being refuelled from a Boeing Stratotanker while escorted by a pair of F-111 fighter bombers. After studying the aircraft until it disappeared, Chris drew a sketch of the unusual formation.

'I don't claim to have seen the Aurora, as they call it,' says Chris. 'Because I really still don't know what I saw. When a colleague on the rig called me from the deck to 'come and a look at this', he was expecting – because he knew of my knowledge of planes – that I'd be able to recognise it right away.

'When I looked up, I was able to identify the tanker and the F-111s, but was amazed by the triangle – it stopped me dead. It wasn't another F-111, nor was it an F-117; the triangle was too long and had no gaps. After considering and rejecting a Mirage IV, I was totally out of ideas.'

The then 27-year-old expert – from Mauchline in Ayrshire – was amazed that, with all his experience, he could not pin down anything with what he called 'this recognition gift'. It was a new experience for him… 'to be absolutely clueless':

My colleague asked me what was going on. As the formation flew overhead I told him that the big one was a KC-135 Stratotanker, the two on the left were F-111s and… I didn't know what the fourth was. Though it was obvious to me that it was something 'dodgy'. Whether this aircraft was an Aurora is debatable – my background precludes jumping to conclusions based on a single piece of evidence. But what was it? I have now been hunting this 'Snark' for years and have turned up some interesting stuff, but I'm still wondering…

So what could it have been? The theories abound. It wasn't a Mirage IV, as Chris had considered and rejected that. There was some conjecture that it could have been a potential replacement for Lockheed's Mach 3.35-plus SR-71 Blackbird reconnaissance aircraft – in other words, a spy plane able to accelerate up to Mach 6 – three times faster than Concorde – powered by a type of experimental jet engine called a pulse detonation engine. However, the former head of Lockheed's Skunkworks division, Ben Rich, claimed 'Aurora' was a codename for the stealth project which eventually led to the B-2 Spirit. Another possible aircraft, which insiders said could have been seen over the North Sea, was the prototype of a Northrop stealth attack plane. The list of potential candidates goes on and on; and as Chris himself says: 'Before any aircraft eventually makes it to production, something like ten mock-ups and 100 design studies are needed. So it could have been anything.'

However, he is sure he came across 'it' again when in 1991 his attention was drawn to an article in an aviation magazine – which was reporting on how California 'was getting hit by 'air quakes' or sonic booms causing seismic events'. Indeed, as in the UK, there were reported sightings of unidentified aircraft flying over California involving odd-shaped contrails, sonic booms, and related phenomena that suggested the US had developed such an aircraft.

Having another string to his bow – as a geologist – he was fascinated and had to agree with the writer's theory that such quakes were being caused by the passing wakes of a hypersonic plane. Up to that point, his long application to the challenge of identifying what he had seen had yielded nothing. 'I'd been taken up various 'hypersonic' garden paths, but all I ever had was this unidentified aircraft still pictured in my head – but not in any books.' Until…

When he saw the magazine feature's aircraft illustration... of a 'sharp 75 degree delta design', which rather matched his own sketch made after the rig sighting, he immediately thought: 'That's it! That's the one I saw!'

But no name was attached to it, so there was nothing to look up. But Chris Gibson is a patient man, trained to be sceptical. And he is not particularly surprised that nothing tangible of that nature has actually materialised. 'I spent the last decade of the last century hunting this 'Snark' and came to the conclusion that if it hadn't been built, there would have been a very good reason for that. All the technology was there.'

So is he letting go of the dream of identifying The Thing?

'Not exactly,' he says. 'But I won't really believe it until the Americans roll it out, saying "this is it", and I can actually walk up to it and kick its tyres.'

In May 2012, the former Machrihanish airbase was sold by the Ministry of Defence for the grand sum of £1 – to a company owned and controlled by local people hoping to reinvigorate the local economy in and around Campbeltown. With the support of Highlands and Island Enterprise, the Scottish Government and Argyll and Bute Council, the Machrihanish Airbase Community Company's primary dual aim is the attraction of business and the creation of jobs. The 1,000 acre site includes Campbeltown Airport and a wind turbine manufacturing facility.

18

Shot on the Doorstep

WHEN THE DISTINCTIVE pistol whose bullets murdered Alistair Wilson was found in a drain not far from the father of two's house, most people thought that marked the beginning of the end of a particularly bewildering crime puzzle that, for ten frustrating days, had yielded few other clues or promising leads to the perpetrator or his motive.

But they were wrong. Now, 15 years later, Police Scotland's officers are no closer to pinning down the who and why of it. Who would shatter the peace of a small rural Scottish town with the cold-blooded gunning down on his doorstep of what, most agreed, was a fine, gentle young man who had been seeing his children off to bed at the time?

Could the answer to 'why?' have been connected with Alistair Wilson's job as a business banker with the Bank of Scotland in Nairn, on the coastal shoulder of Scotland 15 miles east of Inverness? Was the evil act that devastated the family home on the evening of 28 November 2004, one of an aggrieved customer, or a hit man hired by such a person? At the start, that seemed an obvious explanation; but the longer the head-scratching went on, the more complex and murky the theories became.

Some focused on the banker's own business dealings, as he was about to leave the bank and branch out on his own; others suggested that, being key to other people's business ambitions at the bank, he was being 'persuaded' to help a client; still others mentioned money laundering. Questions were even cast on the validity of the gun found on 8 December 2004 – by council workers cleaning a drain on Seabank Road, about 400 metres from the Wilsons' doorstep in Crescent Road, where 30-year-old Alistair had met his bloody fate.

Forensic analysts had identified the semi-automatic Haenel Suhl Model 1 Schmeisser pistol as the murder weapon and detectives established that it had been made in Germany before the war's end. Did that suggest a foreign killer? Or a former military man? Had it been brought back to Britain as a war trophy by someone with military connections? The .25 calibre bullets used were made by Sellier and Bellot in the Czech Republic between 1983 and 1993.

As the drain was on the left-hand side of a street that led out to the main Inverness road, there was speculation that the gun could have been ditched from a car making its getaway to the Highland capital. And thrown by a passenger.

So, two people might have been involved.

Surely such scraps of rare information could lead at least to the start of a warming trail? But no; the case stayed stubbornly cold, despite the massive police inquiry launched at the time… one of the biggest investigations ever mounted in the Highlands and Islands. Their quarry then as now: a baseball-capped man who rang the family's Crescent Road doorbell and asked for Alistair Wilson by name when his wife, Veronica, opened the door in response that Sunday evening. She later described him as stocky, 5ft 4in to 5ft 8in tall, aged 35–40, wearing a dark blue bomber-style jacket and dark jeans. Enough to go on? Apparently not. Ten years later, detectives had interviewed nearly three thousand people and taken as many statements in their fruitless efforts to hunt down the killer.

At the height of the inquiry, no fewer than 60 officers were involved. DNA samples had been collected from a thousand locals, to compare their saliva with that from a cigarette butt found close to the murder scene. But over the years, the case gradually became remarkable not just for its lingering shock in the normally quiet and douche community but for the very aridity of its progress to a solution. And that despite little matters that might have been expected to push it along.

Such as the little matter of the mysterious envelope that passed between the killer and his victim.

Having spent a happy day as a family walking in Culbin Forest near the sea, Alistair had just enjoyed Sunday dinner with his sons, then aged two and four, and was upstairs in their handsome Victorian house, putting them off to bed – when his wife answered the doorbell and called him down to speak to the man (whom she later described as 'weird'). The banker talked with him for about three minutes before he took a blue A4 envelope into the house and spoke briefly to his wife then returned to the front door. Five minutes later an alarmed Veronica heard three loud cracks, and rushed back to the vestibule to find her husband dying. He had been shot three times at point blank range – once in the body and twice in the head. He died an hour later in hospital.

Police have never disclosed the contents of the envelope, though it was said to have the word 'Paul' scrolled on its front, while some reports asserted that it contained…nothing. Others say it simply disappeared.

While Police Scotland have always kept their official teeth in the case – saying 'we remain open-minded and continue to review all possible scenarios' – over all the years since it happened, there have been ongoing 'breakthroughs' and new theories emanating from armchair detectives everywhere that have all led nowhere. More interesting, of course, has been the contribution of serious outsiders with formidable crime-solving credentials – former Scotland Yard detective Peter Bleksley, for example, who believes Alistair was not meant to die the night he was shot. His view is that the killer went to the house 'to negotiate and not assassinate' and had made the banker an offer 'which he could not refuse but it all went wrong when he did, and consequently paid with his life'. Claiming sources in the legal profession in the Central Belt who knew why Alistair was killed but refused to come forward for fear of losing their own lives, he further prods our curiosity by claiming that one of his sources knows that the key to the mystery is contained (though maybe not literally) in the blue envelope.

Peter Bleksley's words are echoed by a detective who was on the case when Alistair's business connections were being closely analysed:

> It could have been something he refused to get involved in that led to his death. Bear in mind at that time you had people at his level signing off on millions, with little or no audit.

Wilson was co-leader of a business team working with small- and medium-size companies right across the Highlands and Islands. Police always emphasised that the banker himself was not involved in financial malpractice; though touching on that at one point Det Supt Gary Cunningham said:

> We can confirm that investigations into Alistair's personal and professional life have been a focus on the inquiry into his death. These matters remain under review.

And a spokesman for Bank of Scotland said:

We assisted the police with their investigation at the time and, if new enquiries are raised by the police, then we will of course assist them further.

Bleksley, preparing to write a book on the case, spent five days in Nairn when he circulated leaflets among homes and shops appealing for information. He received several calls, one claiming to detail the killer's true intentions. 'This is information from a very credible source who knows all the players,' he said. 'This is not my theory.'

Was this another witness? If so, there were now three – already counting Wilson's wife and one Tommy Hogg – which surely added up to a case for a police e-fit [computer-based Electronic Facial Identification Technique] and the wide distribution of it. Tommy Hogg? He stepped forward quite early in the affair to say he had seen 'an interesting person' minutes before the shooting – and he subsequently helped develop an e-fit of the man with police... which was, to his surprise, never released and distributed. So what exactly had the former community councillor seen?

Hogg told this writer that he and his wife noticed a 'very jumpy but unusually immaculate' man on their bus as it left the bus station on the fateful night:

I've lived in the town all my life and you just don't ex-pect to see someone like that on the bus here. That said, my attention was also drawn to him as he was wearing a cap just like my own; the same sandy colour.

He was so close to us – only two seat rows behind – that I could almost have touched him. And every time I looked at him from the corner of my eye he turned his head away shiftily.

Something definitely didn't seem right about him. He was so agitated but his hair, behind the cap, was incredibly well-groomed. I'll never forget his face... so smooth and well-shaved... I thought he could have been a military man.

He got off the bus and turned left down the Wilsons' street – just minutes before the incident. It was amazingly soon after my wife and I got off the bus that the air was filled with dramatic news about the shooting.

Tommy has become quite disillusioned about lack of appreciation of his story and thinks it has become buried among 'so many stories about the thing these days that just go on and on, so I really don't want to talk about it any more'. But he kept one last blast for the official procedures:

Two policemen were sent from Edinburgh three times to talk to me and I contributed quite thoroughly to that e-fit about which I was more than happy – it was a perfect likeness of the man I saw. So couldn't understand why it wasn't circulated and I never heard another word about it.

He wasn't the only one who didn't understand. Bleksley said:

I think it's very strange an e-fit was never released. Had such an e-fit been produced, even all these years later a process could have been applied to it to give some kind of indication as to how the man in the baseball cap may have aged.

Another impressive outsider of that opinion is David Wilson, professor of criminology at Birmingham City University, who has studied the case. He raised the question of 'why the e-fit was never circulated, especially in light of the fact that it was said to be a good likeness'.

But his claim on BBC Radio Scotland's *John Beattie Show* at the end of 2017 that the man on the bus could have been the killer was rejected by Detective Superintendant Cunningham, who commented:

> The information discussed during the radio show has been in the public domain for some time. An e-fit of a potential suspect was drawn up but officers were able to trace the man concerned. We were able to rule him out of having had any involvement in Alistair's death.

Earlier he had said: 'There is limited detail available about the facial features of the suspect from witnesses and as such, there is not sufficient information to produce an e-fit.' To which, Tommy Hogg later responded: 'I know what I saw, but I don't want to challenge the police.'

The radio show was not as ready to back down, however. Professor Wilson 'revealed' to it that the case was now 'eminently solvable'... not least because he had acquired new information in the form of a package, from someone identified only as 'Nate', who claimed there was an independent witness to the murder on the doorstep of the banker's home and put a name to this person. It had been passed to the police.

But as nothing more seemed to come of it, did that become yet another red herring flapping about before expiring? Without it or any other new factor prompting a further meaningful development, the case 'just never seems to move forward beyond speculation and rumours', as Tommy Hogg finally put it.

Meanwhile, the person who most needs a resolution to it – Veronica Wilson – still lives in the house where her husband died, and remains deeply perplexed by what happened. She told BBC Scotland:

> For us as a family, we need to know why. This is just so senseless. For two young boys – aged two and four – to be left without a dad, that can't be repaired. But a who and why would just make such a difference to us being able to move on.
>
> It's harder the older the boys get. Obviously when they were little they were just told their dad had died, and he wasn't there any more. They're young men now so they just can't understand it… why somebody would do that to their dad and why that somebody's not been caught. Justice is a huge factor and issue that they have. Everyone has supported us…but it's still very horrible for them to realise now, who they are. It's not nice being the banker's widow or the banker's children.

Despite having actually opened the house door to the killer, and watched him walk away after doing the deed, Mrs Wilson added: 'I don't know what sort of person I'm trying to find.'